HOUSTON
classic
MEXICAN
recipes

HOUSTON
classic
MEXICAN
recipes

ERIN HICKS MILLER

PELICAN PUBLISHING COMPANY
GRETNA 2011

The word "Pelican" and the depiction of a pelican are trademarks of Pelican Publishing Company, Inc., and are registered in the U.S. Patent and Trademark Office.

U.S. Patent and Trademark Office

ISBN 9781589808959

Text by Erin Hicks Miller

Edited by Erin Hicks Miller, Jeffrey Linthicum

Photography by William Jones Miller

Artwork by William Jones Miller

Production by William Jones Miller

Layout based on a design by Kit Wohl

Printed in China

Published by Pelican Publishing Company, Inc.

1000 Burmaster Street, Gretna, Louisiana 70053

To Billy, my husband, with whom life is a perpetual pachanga.

CONTENTS

SOUPS & SALADS

Real Guacamole	Yelapa	11
Sopa de Poblano	Molina's	12
Carolyn Farb Guacamole	Mo's – A Place for Steaks	15
Ceviche	Beso	16
Southwest Caesar Salad	Olivette	19
Chicken Tortilla Soup	Pappasito's	20
Mango Jicama Salad	1308 Cantina	23
Turkey Pozole	Spanish Flowers	24
Campechana	Habañeros Mex Grill	27

SMALL BITES

Fish Tacos	La Parranda	28
Crepas de Huitlacoche	Julia's Bistro	31
Camarones Diablos	Teala's	32
Shrimp & Mushroom Quesadilla	Escalante's	35
Flautas de Leah	Romero's Las Brazas	36
Taquitos de Langosta	Hugo's	39
Lamb Barbacoa	Tacos A Go-Go	40
Tacos al Pastor	100% Taquito	43
Queso Flameado	El Meson	44
Crab Meat Tostadas	RDG + Bar Annie	47
Shrimp Tamales	Taco Milagro	48
Sopesitos Especiales	Sabores	51

ENCHILADAS

Poblano Mole Enchiladas	La Guadalupana	53
Morelia Enchiladas	Sylvia's Enchilada Kitchen	54
Lobster Enchiladas	Cyclone Anaya's	57
Verde Chicken Enchiladas	Berryhill Baja Grill	58

ENTREES

Chile Relleno	Irma's	60
Carne Asada	El Tiempo	63
Pork Belly al Pastor Torta	Haven	64
Carnitas	Santos – The Taste of Mexico	67
Chipotle Chicken	Doneraki	68
Carne Guisada	Gringo's Mexican Kitchen	71
Huachinango Veracruzana	Las Ventanas	72
Chipotle Costillas	Lupe Tortilla	75
Steak Burrito	Chuy's	76

Cochinita Pibil	The Original Ninfa's	79
Cabrito Enchilado	El Hidalguense	80
Alambres	Alicia's Mexican Grille	83
Jalapeño Glazed Snapper	Cielo Mexican Bistro	84
Chile en Nogada	Tila's	87

DESSERTS

Ojarascas	El Bolillo Bakery	88
Dos Leches y Canela Flan	Rebecca Masson	91
Sopapillas	Teotihuacan	92

SIDES

Corn Tortillas	100% Taquito	43
Borracho Beans	El Tiempo	63
Flour Tortillas	Teotihuacan	92
Mexican Rice	Teotihuacan	94
Salsa Roja	Tila's	94
Famous Green Salsa	The Original Ninfa's	94
Nopalitos Salad	Solero	94
Calabacitas	Beso	94

DRINKS

Yelapa-Chelada	Yelapa	11
Don Raul Margarita	Molina's	12
Watermelon Margarita	Pappasito's	20
Michelada	1308 Cantina	23
Pica Rita	Habañeros Mex Grill	27
Avocado Margarita	La Parranda	28
Mango Margarita	Escalante's	35
Apricot Sunrise	Hugo's	39
Sangria del Meson	El Meson	44
Paloma Cocktail	RDG + Bar Annie	47
Sangrita	Taco Milagro	48
Agua de Melón	Sabores	51
Skinny Margarita	Cyclone Anaya's	57
Irma's Famous Lemonade	Irma's	60
La Vida Local	Haven	64
Horchata	Doneraki	68
Grapefruit Margarita	The Original Ninfa's	79
White Sangria	Cielo Mexican Bistro	84
Tamarindo Agua Fresca	El Bolillo Bakery	88

INTRODUCTION

Tackling a Mexican cookbook, especially in a city where Mexican restaurants outnumber virtually every other international cuisine, was no easy task. I wanted to represent a wide array of regional authentic Mexican cooking, while being mindful to consider the unique variations that the talented local chefs of Houston bring to the table. I learned, early on, that traditional Mexican food is hugely different than what most people are familiar with. Most modern (and often American-ized) interpretations are fried and smothered in yellow cheese. Yellow cheese and deep-frying are the hallmarks of Tex-Mex, not traditional Mexican cuisine. As one of the owners of Pepe's Mexican Cafe (Corpus Christi, Texas) in the mid 1990s, this distinction was truly a revelation. It turns out I was running a Tex-Mex restaurant for all of those years!

While fresh corn, tomatoes, onion, garlic, rice and beans are staples in virtually every Mexican kitchen, six regions (governed largely by their varied landscapes) typically define the diverse cuisines of Mexico. The coastal Ensenada region in the Northwest is colored by Spanish influence and a vibrant fishing industry. In the Northeast, the Sierra Madre mountains dominate the landscape of the Chihuahua region and the hearty, meaty dishes there contribute largely to the Tex-Mex dishes popular in the Southwest United States. Central Mexico serves as the crossroads of Mexican cuisine and, thanks to an abundance of volcanic soil, is the ideal host for the finicky agave plant - making the area the source of the finest tequila on earth. In the Southwest, the Oaxacan region features the most rugged terrain in the country and cooks survive by making the most of the chiles and beans that grow well there. In the South Central area, the Veracruz region established the first regular trade with Africa and Spain, bringing the plantain, several varieties of nuts and the Spanish olive. And in the Yucatan region, the famed Southeastern peninsula of Mexico, influences from their Caribbean neighbors and their coastal location inspire seafood dishes, sauces, marinades and accompaniments that tend to be sweeter, due to the liberal use of local fruits.

Of course, within each region, there are exceptions to these generalizations and more variations of these dishes exist than I could ever represent in ninety-six pages. But, what I've presented here is a collection of cherished and rare recipes for the finest and Mexican cuisine I could find. Some of the recipes are shockingly easy, others are complex, but you'll enjoy greater success if you follow a few basic rules when cooking. Arrange a time when there are no other distractions.

> ## "EL VIENTRE GOBIERNA LA MENTE."
>
> ### ("THE BELLY RULES THE MIND.")
>
> *-Mexican Proverb*

Read the recipe carefully. Read the recipe again. Gather the ingredients. Avoid substitutions. Assemble the equipment and (this is important) take the time to prep and measure everything into separate bowls and containers before cooking anything. Chefs refer to this procedure as preparing the 'mis en place'. The practice and the phrase are easy to remember if you think of it as having your 'mess in place'.

Beyond that general cooking advice, I learned some invaluable tips and tricks while compiling and home-testing the recipes for this cookbook. Where chiles are concerned (and you will encounter more than you knew existed as you cook your way through this book), always wear rubber gloves and remember that the seeds bear the bulk of the heat. Also, the ribs (or membranes) within all peppers are bitter and should always be carefully removed. Wash your fruits and vegetables, including avocados and other fruits and vegetables that are to be peeled. Many of the recipes require a series of smaller preparations before assembling the the main dish. In these instances, I have used an asterisk (*) to indicate that.

For more tips, serving suggestions, videos of techniques used throughout and detailed background on the recipes and the restaurants from whence they came, visit my website at www.erinhicksmiller.com or check out my blog at www. erinhicksmiller.blogspot.com.

I hope this book will inspire you to try some new things and experience a culture that has made countless contributions to the culinary world. My love of Mexican food has reached new heights... and I hope yours will too.

– Erin Hicks Miller

YELAPA
REAL GUACAMOLE

Chef L.J. Wiley is passionate about guacamole. You'll know that after a single bite of this amazing panzanella-esque rendition. Like a panzanella (an Italian bread and tomato salad,) some chips are mixed in and intended to get a little wet - soaking up the chive oil and juices.

At Yelapa, the mango in this recipe is substituted with seasonal flavor varietals like fennel, black olive, persimmon, blood orange and even cinnamon. So, while their guacamole base is instantly recognizable and uniquely 'Yelap-an', the 'punch' of the dish is always pleasantly unexpected. After mastering this mango version, Wiley encourages you to try switching out this ingredient creatively. But remember, the avocado is the star here... let it shine.

YIELD: 4 TO 6 SERVINGS

2	avocados	4 tablespoons	lime juice
½ cup	mango, cut in ½-inch diamonds	½ cup	fennel, cut in eighths, sliced 1/16-inch thick
4 tablespoons	chive oil*	6 tablespoons	black olive purée*
4 tablespoons	Thai basil, ½-inch rough chop	16	corn tortilla chips
4 tablespoons	shallot, sliced ⅛-inch across the vertical axis	½ teaspoon	salt

Toss all the ingredients except the black olive purée in a bowl. Place a 'smear' of the purée down on a plate and place the salad on top. Drizzle with a little more chive oil. Serve with chips.

CHIVE OIL

1 bunch	chives	⅔ cup	corn oil

Blanch the chives in rapidly boiling salted water for no more than 30 seconds. Remove the chives and submerge into an ice bath to cool completely. Remove the chives from the ice bath and squeeze dry. Give them a rough chop before adding to the blender with the corn oil. Blend on high until puréed and strain through a cheesecloth.

BLACK OLIVE PURÉE

1 cup	black olives	2 tablespoons	olive oil
½ cup	black olive liquid		

Purée all ingredients in a blender until smooth.

YELAPA-CHELADA

YIELD: 24 OUNCES - 12 MICHELADAS

MICHELADA BASE

¼ cup	Meyer lemon juice
½ cup	orange juice
2 cups	plum tomatoes (canned)
1 cup	prickly pear purée
1	lime, juiced
¼ cup	sugar
¼ teaspoon	salt
½	red jalapeño
1 teaspoon	Patak's lime pickle (Indian food aisle)

Combine all ingredients in a blender and 'buzz' until smooth.

1½ ounces	michelada base
1	beer of choice
1	lime wedge
	salt, for rim

Rim a glass with salt and a lime wedge. Pour michelada base in bottom of glass. Tilt glass and fill with beer. Serve with remaining beer on the side.

DON RAUL MARGARITA

YIELD: 1 SERVING

1¼ ounces	Don Julio tequila
¾ ounce	Grand Gala orange liqueur
3 ounces	fresh lime
dash	fresh sweet & sour*

Mix all ingredients in a shaker with plenty of ice. Shake for at least 20 seconds. Salt rim. Enjoy!

FRESH SWEET & SOUR

1	lime, juiced
½	lemon, juiced
½ ounce	simple syrup

Combine all ingredients.

MOLINA'S
SOPA DE POBLANO

This hearty and warming cream of poblano soup with roasted corn is topped with jalapeño sausage slices and is a remarkable vehicle for this pepper. You will need between four and five poblanos for this recipe. It's most important not to over-roast the poblanos. You want a bright, slightly roasted pepper or your soup will be dull. Molina's uses Holmes' Smokehouse Jalapeño Sausage to top the soup, which, in my opinion, is the best.

I learned a lot about peppers while compiling this book and have a new appreciation for all varieties. They offer great health, dietary and medicinal benefits. Some varieties are referred to by one name when fresh and another when dried (the jalapeño becomes a chipotle, the poblano becomes an ancho or a mulato) while some, like the chile de arbol and the habañero, are referred to by the same name when fresh or dried. Roasted, fresh peppers will keep in your freezer for up to nine months and dried peppers, if stored in a cool, dark place, will keep for at least as long.

YIELD: 8 SERVINGS

4 tablespoons	butter, salted		½ cup	yellow onion, diced
2 tablespoons	flour		½ cup	poblano pepper, diced
1 pint	chicken stock		⅓ cup	red bell pepper, diced
1 cup	heavy cream		1⅓ tablespoons	cilantro, chopped
1⅛ cups	poblano peppers (about 3)		1 tablespoon	salt
			½ tablespoon	black pepper
2 tablespoons	canola olive oil blend		2 tablespoons	lime juice
3	corn on the cob, roasted & removed from cob		1 pound	jalapeño sausage, smoked, sliced & halved

Roast the poblano peppers under the broiler, just long enough to blister the skin slightly. Remove the peppers from the oven and place in a plastic bag or in a covered container to steam and loosen the skin. Remove the skin and seeds with a paring knife. Place the roasted peppers in a blender and process. Set aside.

Melt the butter in a pan over medium heat. Add the flour and stir. Add the chicken stock slowly and whisk to ensure no lumps. Cook over low heat for 10 to 15 minutes.

Add the heavy cream and the blended poblanos and cook for an additional 10 minutes. Remove from heat and allow to cool slightly.

For the garnish, add olive oil to a pan over medium high heat. Add the onion and cook for about 1 minute. Add the diced poblano, red pepper and roasted corn and cook until the vegetables are soft. Add the cilantro, salt, black pepper, lime juice and the cream and poblano mixture from above.

Top each bowl of soup with a handful of the sausage and serve.

MO'S - A PLACE FOR STEAKS
CAROLYN FARB GUACAMOLE

Not only is Mo's a place for big, flavorful steaks, it turns out that it's also a place for fantastic guacamole.

The key to making perfect guacamole starts with the avocado. Choose avocados that 'give' a little when given pressure with the thumb and forefinger. Taste, taste, taste before serving. The flavor of the fruit (yes, avocados are fruit) can vary wildly depending on its growing season and climate, so adjust the seasoning and lime juice accordingly. Lastly, always remember that the avocado needs to play the starring role... don't let your supporting players upstage it.

YIELD: 4 TO 6 SERVINGS

GUACAMOLE

4	avocados		¼ cup	guacamole relish*
2	limes, juiced		to taste	salt & pepper
2 teaspoons	spice mix*			

Carefully cut the avocados in half and remove the seed.

Scoop out the flesh with a spoon and put into a mixing bowl. Using a fork, slightly mash the avocados. Add the lime juice, the spice mix, and the relish along with salt and pepper to taste. The guacamole should be creamy, buttery and a little chunky. Serve with crispy flour tortilla or wonton chips.

SPICE MIX

1 tablespoon	garlic, granulated		¾ teaspoon	celery salt
¾ teaspoon	onion powder		¾ teaspoon	cumin, ground
⅓ teaspoon	cayenne			

Add all the ingredients to a small bowl or shaker and mix well.

GUACAMOLE RELISH

¼ cup	red onion, small dice		1 tablespoon	serrano, seeded, small dice
1 tablespoon	cilantro, chopped			

Mix all the ingredients in a small bowl.

Native Texan Carolyn Farb, this dish's namesake, is Houston's First Lady of Philanthropy. Her fundraising genius is legendary around the world and she has a gift for inspiring others. Chef Eric Aldis was inspired by the beauty's love for the avocado and his buttery, rich and chunky twist on classic guacamole is a bestseller. When I contacted Carolyn about the recipe, she was quick to point out, "Chef Eric outdid himself and gave it a unique spin with the wonton chips." I couldn't agree more.

Known largely for producing the tastiest steaks and chops available in the Space City, Chef Eric Aldis has solidified his reputation in Houston as a man who knows how to bring big flavor. The award-winning chef cut his culinary teeth at Houston's Four Seasons Hotel before showcasing his talents in nationally recognized eateries like Ritz-Carlton New Orleans, Bellagio and Melange. The award-winning menu there also features sinfully delicious desserts, like the half-baked chocolate chip cookie, which Mo's owner John A. Vassallo was generous enough to share in my Houston Classic Desserts book (Pelican Publishing 2010.)

THE PASSION OF FOOD AND DRINK

Beso was the brainchild of partners Chef Arturo Boada and Bill Sadler. They began their partnership at Solero, a tapas bar, in the late 1990s and are currently 'wow-ing' diners at their newest eatery, Arturo's Uptown Italiano.

I celebrated my 33rd, 34th and 35th birthdays at Beso and I so miss the restaurant, all the good times and especially the great food! I am fortunate enough to be good friends with Chef Arturo and sometimes, if I ask really sweetly, he'll whip up one of my old favorites.

BESO
CEVICHE

The origins of ceviche are sketchy and regularly disputed among fans. It is commonly found throughout the coastal regions of Central and South America, but didn't make its way onto American menus until the 1980s. Traditionally, it contains very fresh, raw fish marinated in lemon or lime juice and tossed with onion, salt, and chile peppers. This version is brightened by the addition of orange juice and passion fruit purée.

YIELD: 2 TO 4 SERVINGS

2 pounds	shrimp, large	¼ cup	red onion, small dice
1	bay leaf	¼ cup	red bell pepper, small dice
½	lemon		
handful	black peppercorns	2 tablespoons	jalapeño, diced
2	snapper fillets	pinch	cumin, ground
1 tablespoon	olive oil	½ teaspoon	salt
2 tablespoons	orange juice	1 tablespoon	cilantro, chopped
2 tablespoons	white vinegar	1 tablespoon	passion fruit purée
½ cup	lime juice, fresh		

Peel and devein the shrimp. Cut each shrimp into 3 or 4 pieces, whatever your preference.

Fill a stock pot half full of water and place on the stove over high heat. Add a bay leaf, half of a lemon and the peppercorns.

When the water starts to boil, add the shrimp and cook for 1 minute. Remove from heat and strain. Transfer the shrimp to a sheet pan, cover with foil or plastic wrap and immediately put into the refrigerator to chill. **DO NOT PUT SHRIMP IN ICE WATER TO CHILL**.

Rinse the snapper filets and make sure that all the skin and scales have been removed. Cut the fish into bite-sized pieces or smaller, to your liking.

In a medium bowl, combine and mix the olive oil, orange juice, white vinegar, lime juice, onion, bell pepper, jalapeño, cumin, salt, cilantro and passion fruit purée. Then add the snapper and the cooled shrimp. Marinate for at least 2 hours, in the refrigerator.

Serve over a bed of greens with plantain or tortilla chips.

Recipe Note: Passion fruit purée may be found in the frozen fruit section of the grocery store.

OLIVETTE
Southwest Caesar Salad

You are undoubtedly surprised to see a Caesar Salad in a Mexican cookbook. Don't be. It was actually created at a Tijuana hotel restaurant, not far from the California border in the 1920s. Its popularity was explosive. Hordes of Californians, including notable celebrities like Clark Gable, Jean Harlow and W.C. Fields, would make the trek to Tijuana just to experience the culinary marvel, which was prepared tableside by Chef Caesar Cardini.

This beloved version by former chef, and now general manager, Jim Mills puts a regional twist on the classic. Walk through the Olivette dining room at any given time and you will see this dish on many tables.

Olivette, at the posh Houstonian Hotel, Club & Spa, is a perfect backdrop for Chef Jeff Everts' classically prepared food.

Beautiful views of the hotel's sprawling green lawns and trees, with fresh flowers at each table, create an atmosphere that makes dining here romantic and memorable.

Appetizers like the fire-roasted mussels and entrees like the Berkshire Pork Tenderloin, with a warm smoked bacon and sherry vinaigrette, and the snapper, with chorizo, black olives and fennel, are reflections of Chef Everts' creativity in the kitchen.

YIELD: 4 SERVINGS

2 heads	romaine lettuce		1½ cups	corn tortilla strips, fried or baked crisp
¾ cup	black beans, cooked		1 cup	southwest caesar dressing*
¾ cup	corn kernels, roasted			
½ cup	pumpkin seeds (pepitas), roasted			
½ cup	Cotija cheese, crumbled			

Wash and spin the lettuce. Trim into 1½-inch pieces. Put the lettuce in a large salad bowl.

Add the beans, corn, pumpkin seeds, most of the cheese and about half the tortillas.

Toss well, then add the dressing and toss again to mix. Taste and correct the seasoning, if necessary.

Divide the salad among 4 service plates. Top with the remaining cheese and sprinkle with the remaining tortilla strips. Serve immediately.

SOUTHWEST CAESAR DRESSING

1	egg yolk		¼ cup	cold water
1 tablespoon	garlic, minced		½ cup	extra virgin olive oil
1 tablespoon	dijon mustard		½ cup	canola oil
3	anchovy filets, minced		1½ tablespoons	Sambal chili paste (Thai chili paste)
1½ teaspoons	black pepper, ground		½ teaspoon	lemon, juiced
¼ teaspoon	salt		½ teaspoon	lime, juiced
½ teaspoon	cumin, ground		¼ cup	parmesan cheese, grated fine
½ teaspoon	coriander, ground			
1 teaspoon	worcestershire sauce			

Combine the egg yolk, garlic, mustard, anchovy, pepper, salt, cumin, coriander, worcestershire and water in the work bowl of a food processor fitted with a steel blade.

Process until smooth, then add the oil, bit by bit, until the emulsion forms and the sauce has thickened. When all of the oil has been incorporated, add the chili paste, citrus juices and cheese. Process until smooth and taste to adjust the seasoning, if necessary.

WATERMELON MARGARITA

YIELD: 1 SERVING

6 (1-inch)	watermelon squares, fresh
1½ ounces	silver tequila
½ ounce	watermelon liqueur
2 ounces	fresh sweet & sour*

In a mixing glass, muddle the fresh watermelon for 5 seconds. Add the tequila, watermelon liqueur and fresh sweet and sour. Fill with ice and shake for 10 seconds.

Garnish with a watermelon wedge.

FRESH SWEET & SOUR

1	lime, juiced
½	lemon, juiced
½ ounce	simple syrup

Combine all ingredients.

PAPPASITO'S
CHICKEN TORTILLA SOUP

This has been my favorite tortilla soup for over a decade. The fresh squash, zucchini, tomatoes and jalapeños are combined with corn, onions and chunky grilled chicken breast and topped with tortilla strips, avocado and cheese. You may substitute shredded chicken for the strips and a rotisserie chicken is a real time-saver.

YIELD: 6 SERVINGS

10 cups	chicken broth, low sodium	to taste	salt & pepper
2 cups	yellow onions, julienned	for frying	oil
2 cups	carrots, half moon, sliced ⅓-inch thick	6 (3-inch)	corn tortillas, cut into ¼-inch strips
1 tablespoon	jalapeños, minced	¾ pound	chicken, grilled, ½-inch dice
1 tablespoon	chicken boullion		
2 cups	zucchini, quartered, sliced ½-inch thick	¾ pound	Monterey Jack cheese, shredded
2 cups	yellow squash, quartered, sliced ½-inch thick	1	avocado, peeled, seeded, 1-inch dice
2 cups	tomatoes, 1-inch rough chop	sprinkle	paprika
		6	cilantro sprigs
1½ cups	corn kernels, fresh, from 2 ears	1	lime, cut into 6 wedges

Place the chicken broth in a stock pot or dutch oven over medium-high heat and bring to a boil. Lower the heat to medium and add the onions, carrots, jalapeños and chicken bouillon to the stock.

Cook for about 15 minutes or until the carrots are half done (still firm without crunch.) Add the zucchini, squash, tomatoes and fresh corn kernels. Simmer for an additional 10 minutes. Season to taste with salt and pepper.

For the fried tortilla strips, heat the oil in a heavy pot or electric fryer to 350°F. Add the tortilla strips in batches and fry until golden and crisp, 1½ to 2 minutes. Remove with a slotted spoon and allow excess oil to drain on paper towels. Season with salt.

To serve, ladle the soup broth into 6 bowls, reserving 1 cup. Divide the chicken, cheese and avocado evenly among the bowls. Sprinkle with paprika. Pour remaining 1 cup of soup broth over the top. Garnish each bowl with fried tortilla strips, a cilantro sprig and a lime wedge.

1308 CANTINA
Mango Jicama Salad

The soft mango and crunchy jicama make this unique salad a textural delight. It's a perfect dish with a tangy twist for someone looking to eat light and healthy. Quite versatile, it is delicious topped with chicken, dry chili powder or even with a side of whipped cream. Just make sure to always use fresh fruit.

YIELD: 4 TO 6 SERVINGS

2	mangos	½ teaspoon	black pepper
2	jicamas	½ teaspoon	salt
½ cup	frozen orange juice concentrate	1 to 2 tablespoons	water

Slice the jicama into rounds and then julienne. Slice the mango into similar sized pieces. Put the jicama and mango into a large bowl.

Scoop out the orange juice concentrate and add to a small bowl or squeeze bottle. Add the pepper, salt and water. Shake or whisk to combine. Add more water to your desired consistency.

Pour the mixture over the mango and jicama and toss.

Top with pomegranate seeds or diced strawberries. Cilantro leaves may also be added for color.

MICHELADA

YIELD: 12 MICHELADAS

10 ounces	lime juice, fresh
3½ tablespoons	worchestershire
½ teaspoon	soy sauce
10 ounces	hot sauce (Cajun Chef)
¼ teaspoon	black pepper
⅔ teaspoon	Maggi sauce*
12	beers of choice
optional	Tabasco

Mix all the ingredients (except the beer) together. Use 2 ounces of mix per beer. If you like it spicy, add a dash of Tabasco.

TIP: If you can't find Maggi sauce, you may substitute equal parts of soy and worchestershire.

TURKEY POZOLE

This is a very traditional dish with pre-Columbian history. Colorful, spicy and hearty yet light, this soup is often served at Christmas or on special occasions. This is also the base for the more exotic traditional soup menudo, which uses tripe (cow stomach or intestines) instead of turkey. Many claim that menudo is the very best hangover cure available, so this recipe is a similarly effective alternative for someone who can't 'stomach' tripe.

YIELD: 8 TO 10 SERVINGS

5	guajillo chiles, seeded		2 cups	water
1	ancho, small, seeded			

In a frying pan over medium heat, stir fry the chiles quickly so as not to burn (about 30 seconds). Remove from the skillet. Soak the chiles in the water for 2 hours.

½ (12 pound)	turkey		2 tablespoons	vegetable oil
4 quarts	water		1 (36 oz.) can	white hominy, rinsed & drained
1	carrot, chopped			
½	onion, medium, chopped		½	green cabbage, medium, shredded
2	celery stalks, chopped			
2 teaspoons	salt		8	radishes, diced
½ tablespoon	cumin, whole		1	onion, medium, diced
2	garlic cloves		2	avocados, diced
1	tomato, medium			

Cut the turkey at the breast joint and at the leg and thigh joints and rinse well. Place the turkey in a large stockpot.

Add the water, carrot, onion, celery, salt and cumin. Cook on medium heat for 1 hour and 30 minutes or until tender.

Skim impurities off the top of the stock. Remove the turkey from stock.

Remove skin and cut into bite-sized pieces. Strain the broth and discard the vegetables.

In a blender, purée the chiles, garlic and tomato with 2 cups of the broth. Set aside.

Add the oil to a large stockpot. Heat the oil to medium high, add the blended chiles and stir.

Quickly add the remaining broth to the chiles.

Next, add the turkey meat and hominy. Bring to a low boil and cook for 5 to 7 minutes. At this time you may add more salt if desired. Remove from the heat and serve.

Garnish each serving with ½ cup shredded cabbage. Top the cabbage with the radish, onion and avocado.

Open 24 hours a day for over thirty years now, chef and owner Mary Bernal's "hands on" approach guarantees the same consistent and delicious food at noon, midnight or 3am. In fact, the only time she and the restaurant take a break is on Tuesday nights. They close at 10pm and then reopen on Wednesday morning at 9am.

Accolades are never ending for Spanish Flowers-"Best Mexican Food", "Best Late Night Dining", "Best Margaritas" and several of the late Marvin Zindler's "Cleanest Kitchen in the City" awards grace the walls there. Additionally, the Zagat Survey has named Spanish Flowers a "Heights Neighborhood Legend" many years in a row.

Specialties on the menu include caldo de rez, lengua (beef tongue), mole poblano (my nemesis) and menudo. Every week they make over 300 pounds of menudo!

HABAÑEROS MEX GRILL
CAMPECHANA

Renowned Chef Polo Becerra is widely-known for his Post Oak Grill and Polo's Signature restaurants. Not surprisingly, his newest concept, Habañeros Mex Grill, was a very much anticipated addition to the fold. He did not disappoint. The beautiful 4,000 square foot Midtown location features indoor and patio dining and, as expected, a menu that makes your mouth water. A second location in the Uptown area is sure to please as well. This version of Campechana, a famous Mexican Seafood cocktail, features shrimp, calamari and scallops - but squeamish cooks can use just shrimp if they are so inclined.

YIELD: 2 TO 4 SERVINGS

1 cup	shrimp	3	cilantro sprigs, chopped
½ cup	calamari		
1 cup	scallops	½ cup	lime juice
4 cups	water	¼ cup	orange juce
¼ cup	red onion, chopped	1½ cups	ketchup
1 to 2	jalapeños, minced	to taste	salt & pepper

Peel and devein the shrimp. Chop the calamari and scallops into bite-sized pieces.

In a large stockpot, bring the water to a boil. Add the shrimp, calamari and scallops.

Cook for 2 to 3 minutes, then strain.

In a large bowl, mix the red onion, jalapeño, cilantro, lime juice, orange juice and ketchup. Add salt and pepper to taste.

Next, add the shrimp, calamari and scallops. Mix well.

Serve in a glass container and garnish with sliced avocado. Top with a few cilantro sprigs.

PICA RITA

Chamoy is a Mexican condiment made from pickled fruit. It is salty, sweet, sour, and spicy and may be found in liquid or paste form.

YIELD: 4 SERVINGS

¼ cup	chamoy
¼ cup	mango purée
½ teaspoon	chile powder
24 ounces	frozen margarita*
	chile powder, for rim

Add the chamoy, mango purée and chile powder to the frozen margarita recipe below. Blend until smooth. Moisten the rim of the glasses with a lime wedge and dip into a plate of chile powder. Pour into the glasses and enjoy.

FROZEN MARGARITA

3 to 4 cups	ice
6 ounces	tequila
6 ounces	frozen limeade concentrate
2 ounces	triple sec

Add all ingredients to a blender, and purée until smooth.

AVOCADO MARGARITA

YIELD: 6 SERVINGS

2 cups	ice
6 ounces	tequila
4 ounces	lime juice, fresh
3 ounces	triple sec
1	avocado

Place the ice, tequila, lime juice and triple sec into a blender and purée. Add the avocado and blend until smooth. Pour into margarita or martini glasses to serve.

LA PARRANDA
FISH TACOS

My husband, a self-proclaimed fish taco connoisseur, has his favorites all across the United States. He believes these colorful, grilled fish tacos are the best in Houston, or anywhere for that matter.

Other standouts on the menu include the Spinach Portabello Quesadilla and the Poblano en Crema.

YIELD: 24 TACOS

FISH

8 (5 to 7 oz.)	tilapia or snapper fillets		¼ cup	butter, unsalted
¼ cup	garlic, granulated		24	corn or flour tortillas
1 tablespoon	salt		2	avocados, large

Season the fish fillets with the garlic and salt. In a saucepan, heat the butter over medium-high heat and add the fish. Cook for just a few minutes per side, or until the fish flakes easily with a fork.

Warm the tortillas and cut the avocados in slices.

Cut the sautéed fillets into 3 pieces. Place one third of a fillet onto a tortilla, add some of the red cabbage slaw, an avocado slice and top with the mayo-chipotle sauce. Repeat with remaining tortillas.

Serve with charro beans.

RED CABBAGE SLAW

½	red cabbage		1 teaspoon	sugar
½ cup	olive oil		1 teaspoon	salt
½ cup	white vinegar		1 teaspoon	garlic, granulated

Finely shred the cabbage and place it in a bowl.

Add the olive oil, vinegar, sugar, salt and garlic. Toss well and refrigerate for 2 hours to allow the flavors to blend.

MAYO-CHIPOTLE SAUCE

½ cup	mayonnaise	1 to 2 tablespoons	chipotles (canned)

Add the mayo and whole chipotles into the blender and purée. Keep the sauce refrigerated.

JULIA'S BISTRO
CREPAS DE HUITLACOCHE

This recipe features what is probably the most exotic ingredient you will come across in this book - huitlacoche. Often referred to as the Mexican Truffle, a term coined by the James Beard Foundation, this mushroom-like fungus grows between the husk and the kernel on ears of corn. The flavor is best described as mushroom-like, sweet, savory, woody and earthy. Available canned or frozen, many online gourmet suppliers offer it. Surprisingly, I found it at my local grocer in the international food aisle.

YIELD: 6 CREPES

1 tablespoon	olive oil		12 (6-inch)	crepe shells*
¼ cup	tomatoes, small dice		1 cup	Panela cheese, crumbled
1 tablespoon	garlic, minced		to top	cream sauce*
¾ cup	huitlacoche			
to taste	salt & pepper			

Heat the olive oil in a medium sauté pan over medium-high heat. Add the tomatoes and garlic. Cook for 1 to 2 minutes. Next, add the huitlacoche. Add salt and pepper to taste. Cook for an additional 5 minutes, stirring gently along the way.

Add 1 tablespoon each of the huitlacoche mixture and crumbled cheese to one quarter of a crepe. Fold the crepe in half and then in half again. Repeat this procedure with the remaining crepe shells.

CREPE SHELLS

2 cups	flour		¼ teaspoon	salt
2 cups	milk		2 tablespoons	butter, unsalted
2	eggs			

In a medium mixing bowl, whisk together the flour, milk, eggs and salt.

Heat a large frying pan or wok over medium high heat. When the pan is hot, add a teaspoon of butter and lightly coat the surface of the pan with the melted butter.

Pour ¼ cup of the batter into the pan and tilt the pan with a circular motion so that the batter coats the surface in a smooth and even layer.

After 2 minutes, lift up an edge of the crepe with a spatula to see if it is browning. When the underside has begun to brown, flip the crepe and cook the other side until it is also browned, about 2 minutes.

Repeat the same steps with the remaining butter and batter to make 6 crepes. Best served hot.

Julia's Bistro is a really unique dining experience. The menu there is filled with an amazing array of dishes that fuse traditional Latin flavors with modern cooking techniques. Even the most discriminating foodie would be intrigued by their Filete de Pargo en Platanos Verdes - a plantain-crusted snapper filet with a ginger-mango butter sauce or the Costillar de Cordero - a potato-crusted and garlic-stuffed rack of lamb with a vanilla-merlot reduction.

CREAM SAUCE

¼ cup	mozzarella cheese, shredded
½ cup	heavy cream
pinch	salt & pepper

Combine the heavy cream and mozzarella chesse in a saucepan over medium high heat until boiling. Add salt and pepper to taste. Cook for about 3 more minutes and remove from heat.

Spoon the sauce over the crepes and serve.

TEALA'S
CAMARONES DIABLOS

The buttery marinade on these bacon-wrapped, jalapeño-stuffed jumbo shrimp takes this classic dish to another level. Keep your eye on them once they hit the grill... the shrimp will cook very quickly.

YIELD: 2 TO 4 SERVINGS

1	jalapeños	1 teaspoon	garlic powder
12	shrimp, jumbo	½ tablespoon	olive oil
6 to 12	bacon slices	1	yellow onions, large
¼ cup	soy sauce	1	green or red bell pepper
2 tablespoons	butter, unsalted		

Fire up your grill, mesquite wood preferable.

First wash, then very thinly slice the jalapeños length-wise into 12 strips.

Clean, peel and devein the shrimp. Place a slice of jalapeño in the same area from which the vein was removed. Wrap ½ to 1 slice of bacon around each shrimp. Repeat with the remaining shrimp. You may secure the bacon with toothpicks or thread the shrimp onto skewers, which will make handling them on the grill much easier.

Melt the butter, add the garlic powder and stir to combine.

In a shallow dish, combine half of the soy sauce and the garlic butter and marinate the shrimp for 30 minutes.

Thinly slice the onions and bell pepper and set aside.

Remove the shrimp from the marinade and grill for 3 to 5 minutes.

In a skillet over medium heat, sauté the onion and bell pepper in the olive oil and add the remaining soy sauce to the pan.

Place the grilled shrimp on top of the onions and bell peppers and serve.

Recipe Note: Thin, rather than thick bacon, works best here.

During a journey to Mexico's Yucatan peninsula, owners Teal and Surin Anomaiprasert, natives of Thailand, experienced vast similarities between Thai and Mexican cuisine. Upon their return to the U.S., they began to conceptualize a Mexican fusion restaurant and bar to add to their coterie of popular Thai eateries. Favored menu items there include their unique black bean dip and cochinita pibil with a sweet Thai-inspired twist.

The restaurant itself is something of a landmark in Houston. The elevated patio has been a coveted hangout since opening in 1993 and the large oak tree growing through the restaurant features unusual finds it has swallowed up while growing.

ESCALANTE'S
SHRIMP & MUSHROOM QUESADILLA

The quesadilla is thought to have originated in the Oaxaca region as a treat that showcased the amazing mozzarella-esque cheese from the area. For this delicious version, you can use Oaxaca, mozzarella, Monterey Jack, chihuaua or quesadilla cheese. The shrimp called for in this recipe are 31/35s, which just means there are 31 to 35 shrimp per pound. Use larger or smaller, if you like.

Escalante's Chef Rodrigo Juarez is a stickler when it comes to fresh ingredients and fans of the upscale eatery say it's what makes the difference. The chile con queso fresco, the guacamole, prepared table-side and the amazing tenderloin fajitas are among the favorite menu items of these die-hards. Juarez encourages you to use the freshest shrimp available when recreating this recipe and reminds you to not overcook the shrimp or the spinach - both need to be 'babied' in the pan and never left unattended while on the heat.

YIELD: 2 QUESADILLAS

1 tablespoon	butter		4	flour tortillas, large
½ cup	mushrooms		1 cup	white cheese, shredded
2	garlic cloves, minced			
2 cups	spinach, fresh			
14	shrimp, shelled & deveined (31/35)			

Heat the butter in a sauté pan over medium heat. Add the mushrooms and garlic and cook until soft.

Next, add the spinach to the pan along with the shrimp. Cook until the spinach is soft and shrimp are pink (about 1½ to 2 minutes.)

Place each tortilla on a flat grill over medium heat. Top each tortilla with ½ cup of the cheese and let cook until the cheese melts.

Add the ingredients from the sauté pan to 2 of the tortillas.

Take the other tortillas and place on top.

Cut each quesadilla into 6 triangles.

Serve with guacamole, pico de gallo and sour cream.

MANGO MARGARITA

YIELD: 1 SERVING

1½ ounces	100% agave silver tequila
¾ ounce	triple sec liqueur
1½ ounces	simple syrup
¾ ounce	lime juice, fresh
2 ounces	mango purée, fresh

Combine all the ingredients into a shaker with ice. Shake vigorously for 10 seconds. Serve in a salt-rimmed glass. Garnish with cut mango.

THE REAL MEXICAN DEAL

Chef Mama Celia is responsible for almost all of the recipes at Romero's Las Brazas. The menu there features many award-winning dishes, most inspired by the Oaxacan region of Southwest Mexico. But influences from all over Mexico appear on the menu. Their Pambazo Chilango is a dish which has roots in Veracruz. It's a 'sandwich' made with Mexican bread that is first brushed with chile sauce and then grilled. Then, they add a smidge of refried beans, their Teresita stuffing of potatoes and chorizo and a sprinkling of crumbled queso fresco. If I could be alone in a room with this sandwich, it wouldn't be pretty.

Manuel and Leah opened Romero's Las Brazas in May of 2003. Rave reviews, from critics and diners alike, made opening a second location a 'no-brainer'. Mama Celia, sister Lucia and brother Ignacio all play key roles in the operation, making this a family tradition of exceptional cuisine that never disappoints. Love and passion are the secret ingredient in the kitchens of the Romero family restaurants - something Mama Celia encourages you to remember when recreating this flauta recipe.

ROMERO'S LAS BRAZAS
FLAUTAS DE LEAH

This is a super simple recipe made with fresh ingredients that are available to everyone and can fit anyone's budget. The flavor combination is irresistible and you will find yourself wanting more and more as you eat them. It's a dish that proves the point - recipes don't have to be extensive and complicated to produce something incredible.

YIELD: 20 TO 25 FLAUTAS

2½ pounds	chicken breast	½ tablespoon	cumin, ground
1 tablespoon	salt	20 to 25	corn tortillas
1 tablespoon	vegetable oil	for frying	vegetable oil
½	onion, sliced	for garnish	queso fresco, crumbled
1 pound	tomatoes, quartered		
1 tablespoon	Knorr chicken boullion		
¼ cup	chipotles, (canned), blended		

Put the chicken in a stockpot with the salt and cover with water. Bring to a boil then reduce the heat to medium. Simmer for 8 to 10 minutes. Drain the water and let the chicken cool. Shred the chicken and set aside.

In a deep skillet, heat 1 tablespoon of oil over medium heat and add the onion. Cook for 2 to 3 minutes, then add the tomatoes and cook for an additional 2 to 3 minutes.

Add the chicken bouillon, chipotles and cumin. Stir to combine. Then add the chicken and stir for a few minutes more. Remove from the heat and drain any excess liquid.

Next, heat a little oil in a skillet over medium high heat. Quickly warm each tortilla on both sides. Add a little of the chicken mixture, then roll and secure with a toothpick. Next, add few inches of oil to a dutch oven or stockpot. Heat the oil to 350°F and fry each flauta for 2 to 3 minutes or until golden brown. Drain excess grease on a paper towel-lined plate.

Quickly top with queso fresco. Serve with guacamole salsa and sides of your choice.

GUACAMOLE SALSA

¼ pound	tomatillos	6 tablespoons	cilantro
2 to 3	avocados	½ to 1 cup	water
6 tablespoons	onion	to taste	salt
2 cloves	garlic		

Combine all the ingredients and blend to desired consistency.

HUGO'S
Taquitos de Langosta

This dish was inspired by the the lobster dinners Chef Hugo Ortega enjoyed in Ensenada, Mexico. When in season, children sell lobster on the street corners and all the restaurants have special lobster dishes. This combination of lobster, mojo de ajo and black beans is stellar. Hugo's advice for the home cook? Take your time and be patient when sautéeing the garlic. Slow cooking really makes this dish amazing.

YIELD: 12 TAQUITOS

PICO DE GALLO

2	tomatoes, finely diced	½	lime, juiced
1	onion, finely diced	1	jalapeño, minced
2 tablespoons	cilantro, finely chopped	pinch	salt

Toss the ingredients together in a medium bowl. Adjust the seasoning as necessary. Set aside.

MOJO DE AJO

½ cup	olive oil	1	chipotle (canned), chopped
10 to 15	garlic cloves, minced	½	lime, juiced

Heat the oil in a large sauté pan over medium heat. Add the garlic and cook slowly until lightly browned and soft, about 20 minutes. Take care not to burn. Add the chipotle and lime juice. Cook for a few minutes more to incorporate.

REFRIED BLACK BEANS

1 cup	black beans, dry	2 tablespoons	lard
¼	white onion, sliced	to taste	kosher salt
3 cups	water		

Bring the beans, onion and water to a boil. Simmer until the beans are soft, 1 to 2 hours. Strain and reserve the liquid. Blend or mash the beans with a little of the reserved liquid. Heat the lard in a skillet, add the beans and refry over medium-low heat until black and shiny, about 30 minutes. Add a little of the reserved bean water if the beans get too dry.

LOBSTER

1½ pounds	lobster meat, cut into 2-inch pieces	2	avocados, thinly sliced
12 (3-inch)	tortillas		

Add 2 tablespoons of the mojo de ajo to a medium skillet over medium heat. Add the lobster in 6-piece batches, turning occasionally until fully cooked. This will not take too long. Repeat with the remaining mojo de ajo and lobster.

Warm the tortillas in a dry hot pan. To assemble the taquitos, add a smidge of beans to each of the tortillas, add 2 pieces of lobster, garnish with a little pico de gallo, an avocado slice and top with a little mojo de ajo.

APRICOT SUNRISE

YIELD: 1 SERVING

1½ ounces	Don Julio Reposado tequila
¾ ounce	Rothman Apricot liqueur
1 ounce	Alta Vista Torrontes wine
1 ounce	lime juice, fresh
1	orange wedge, juiced
1	egg white

Combine the ingredients in a shaker and shake well for 15 seconds.

Add a small scoop of ice and shake again vigorously for 30 seconds. Strain into a stemless wine glass.

GARNISH

1 teaspoon	peach marmalade
dash	orange bitters

Garnish with the marmalade and a dash of orange bitters.

Barbacoa sounds exotic, until you realize that the technique would evolve into a popular American cooking passion - barbecue. In Mexican cooking culture, barbacoa is thought to be derived from the Spanish-colonized, Carribean island of Barbados. There, the leaves of the Bearded Fig Tree are used to wrap meats before laying them in firepits that are then covered with earth.

While barbacoa is not exclusive to any particular protein, die-hard fans of the dish often prefer to use the head of cattle or lamb - specifically the tender and delicate cheek and temple meat. In the Yucatan region, pork is the protein of choice. (See the Cochinita Pibil recipe on page 79.) The use of lamb is thought to be common in the central Jalisco region of Mexico.

Considered a specialty meat, some restaurants and markets only sell barbacoa on weekends or holidays, due in large part to the elaborate preparation required when using a pit.

Tacos a Go-Go serves barbacoa daily, along with other award winners, like their Verde and Pollo Guisado tacos.

TACOS A GO-GO
Lamb Barbacoa

Texas Monthly listed this as one of the 'Sixty-Three Tacos to Eat Before You Die' in 2006. One bite and you'll understand why. This version uses lamb and bypasses the traditional cooking method of burying the meat in a firepit but retains all of the authentic flavor that makes it so tasty.

It's a good idea to have your butcher cut the shank in half, or even thirds to fit into your stock pot. I can't suggest strongly enough that you use lamb on the bone. The meat garners loads of flavor from the oils in the bone. While it is a little more expensive... it is completely worth it and borderline addictive!

YIELD: 30 TACOS

12 pounds	lamb shank, on the bone	1 pound	tomatoes, sliced
¼ cup	Tony's seasoning	1	celery bunch, ½-inch dice
1½ tablespoons	salt	3	garlic cloves, whole
3	bay leaves	6	chipotle chiles, dry
10	carrots, ½-inch dice	1½ gallons	water
2	yellow onions, sliced		
1 can	garbanzo beans		

In large bowl, add the lamb and season with Tony's seasoning and salt.

In an extra large stock pot, add the bay leaves, carrots, onions, garbanzo beans, tomatoes, celery, garlic, chipotle peppers and water.

Place a strainer in the pot and put the lamb in the strainer.

Cook over medium heat for 4 hours.

Remove the lamb and shred. Serve in warmed tortillas topped with lettuce, tomato and onion.

Recipe Note: The broth makes for a great soup, just add the shredded lamb and you have a meal complete with lots of yummy vegetables. When testing this recipe, I decided to blend up a few cups of the broth and vegetables. I then added the blended mixture to the shredded lamb and it was delish!

100% TAQUITO
Tacos al Pastor

100% Taquito began in 1996 as a food concession truck created for a school project at the University of Houston. After enjoying phenomenal success (and great marks,) they moved to their current permanent location where they incorporated the 'taco trailer' façade into the structure. The effect mirrors the original intention of the project - to recreate the experience of eating in the streets of Mexico City. So clever and so, so yummy. Pork tenderloin is a wonderful substitute for the butt.

YIELD: 20 TO 25 TACOS

3	bay leaves	3 pounds	pork butt or leg, cut into strips
⅔ cup	white vinegar	1	onion, large
8	guajillo chiles	1 bunch	cilantro
1 teaspoon	oil	3	limes
⅔ cup	pineapple juice	1 can	pineapple tidbits, drained
¾ teaspoon	cumin, ground		
¾ teaspoon	black pepper	1 tablespoon	oil
1 teaspoon	Knorr chicken boullion	20 to 25	tortillas
1 teaspoon	garlic powder		
1 teaspoon	salt		

Blend the bay leaves with the vinegar and strain the solution.

In a skillet over high heat, toast the guajillo chiles in the oil for no longer than a minute. Remove the chiles from the oil and soak them in the vinegar until soft.

Blend the chiles in vinegar along with the pineapple juice, cumin, black pepper, chicken bouillon, garlic powder and salt. Marinate the pork in the guajilllo mixture for at least 8 hours, preferably overnight, in the refrigerator.

Chop the onions and cilantro and place in separate dishes. Cut the limes into wedges. In a separate skillet brown the pineapple tidbits.

Warm your choice of oil in a large skillet, over high heat. Once hot, add the strips of pork and cook until brown, or temperature reaches 160˚F. Let the pork sit for 10 minutes, then cut into smaller pieces.

Warm the corn tortillas in the microwave or in a skillet. Place a tortilla on a plate, then add some pork and garnish with pineapple tidbits, cilantro, onions and salsa verde.

SALSA VERDE

1½ pounds	tomatillos	¼ cup	water
6	serranos	½ teaspoon	garlic powder
1 cup	cilantro leaves	1 teaspoon	salt

Husk and wash the tomatillos and cut into quarters. Wash serranos (remove seeds if you prefer a milder salsa.) Combine all ingredients in a blender and purée. Salsa should be bright green, tangy and spicy. This is a wonderful salsa for tacos and as a condiment for other foods. It is also great for chilaquiles - just heat up the sauce in the microwave and add to chips, cheese, chicken and a little sour cream. Garnish with avocado.

CORN TORTILLAS

YIELD: 16 TORTILLAS

2 cups	Maseca
1⅛ cups	water
¼ teaspoon	salt

Combine the Maseca, water and salt in a medium-sized bowl. Mix thoroughly for a few minutes to form a soft dough. Add more water if necessary to form a play-dough-like consistency.

Divide the dough into 16 equal-shaped balls. Line a tortilla press with a Ziploc bag, split down the sides and zipper removed. Place each ball between the plastic and press down until the tortilla is 6-inches in diameter. Peel off the plastic wrap and place on a flat grill or skillet over medium-high heat. Cook for just under a minute. Flip and cook the other side for about 45 seconds. Keep the tortillas warm with a cloth napkin or in aluminum foil.

SANGRIA DEL MESON

1 liter	red wine
1 liter	orange juice
3	apples
2	oranges
1	lemon
⅓ cup	sugar
4 ounces	Spanish brandy

Stir the sugar into the wine until it dissolves entirely, then add the orange juice and brandy.

Peel and cut the apples, oranges and lemon into small bite-sized pieces and let steep in the wine for at least an hour in the refrigerator.

EL MESON
QUESO FLAMEADO

Not only is queso flameado sinfully delicious, it's also dramatic in its presentation. Just before serving, alcohol is added and set aflame, giving the dish a unique flavor and a memorable visual impact. You may also substitute Mexican brandy for a truly traditional preparation.

This queso flameado is made with Riojano sausage, which is the texture and firmness of a summer sausage - which you may use to substitute in this recipe. Just be sure to remove the casings of either before using.

The Garcia Family opened El Meson in 1981 and it has become a Houston sensation over the years. The combination of Spanish regional cuisines mixed with traditional Cuban and Mexican fare has proven to attract serious foodies who return again and again for the superlative food they produce.

YIELD: 4 SERVINGS

¼ pound	Riojano sausage	to taste	salt & black pepper
½	onion, medium	½ pound	chihuahua cheese
½	red bell pepper	¼ pound	brie cheese
1 tablespoon	olive oil	1 ounce	bourbon
¼ teaspoon	cayenne pepper		

Preheat the oven to 375˚F.

Remove the sausage from its casing and cut it into small ¼-inch cubes.

Chop the onion and bell pepper into ¼-inch cubes.

Heat the olive oil in a skillet, add the onion, bell pepper and sausage and sweat over low heat, about 5 minutes. Add the cayenne pepper and salt and pepper to taste.

Cut both cheeses into small cubes, mix and place in an oven-proof ceramic dish.

Pour the onions, peppers and sausage into the cheese mixture.

Place in the oven and heat for 10 minutes or until melted.

Discard the oil that rose to the top and place the ceramic dish on a serving plate.

Pour the bourbon over the top and light to burn off excess alcohol.

Serve with fresh tortillas.

RDG + BAR ANNIE
CRAB MEAT TOSTADAS

YIELD: 36 TOSTADITOS

AVOCADO RELISH

2	Haas avocados, ½-inch dice	1 tablespoon	extra virgin olive oil
½	serrano, minced	1 teaspoon	lime juice, fresh
¼	white onion, finely slivered	½ teaspoon	salt
¼ cup	cilantro leaves	¼ teaspoon	black pepper, freshly ground

In a small mixing bowl, combine all of the ingredients. Lightly mash or stir with a spoon to achieve a creamy texture. Be careful not to over-mix. Press a piece of plastic wrap onto the surface of the relish and refrigerate.

CRAB MEAT

1 pound	crab meat, jumbo, lump, fresh	2 tablespoons	heavy cream
2 tablespoons	mayonnaise	1 teaspoon	lime juice, fresh
		pinch	salt & pepper

Check and clean the crab meat for any shells. In a medium mixing bowl, combine the mayonnaise and heavy cream and mix until smooth. Add the lime juice, salt, pepper and blend. Add the crab meat and gently toss to lightly coat. Add a little additional heavy cream if necessary to fully coat the crab meat.

CABBAGE SLAW

½	green cabbage, thinly sliced	½	serrano, minced
¼ cup	cilantro sprigs, roughly chopped	1 tablespoon	extra virgin olive oil
4	radishes, thinly sliced	1 teaspoon	lime juice, fresh
		pinch	salt & pepper

Combine all the ingredients in a medium bowl and lightly toss.

TOSTADITOS

12 (6-inch)	corn tortillas	for frying	oil

With a 2½-inch cookie cutter, cut 3 small rounds from each tortilla. Heat an inch of oil in a frying pan to about 350˚F. Lightly fry the tortilla rounds until crisp. Drain on a paper towel. Lightly sprinkle with salt.

ASSEMBLY

for garnish	red fresno chile or jalapeño, thinly sliced into rounds cilantro leaves

To assemble, spread some of the avocado relish on each chip. Spoon some of the crab mixture over the avocado relish. Garnish the crab with a thin slice of chile. Finish each tostada with a small pile of cabbage slaw and a cilantro leaf.

PALOMA COCKTAIL

YIELD: 1 SERVING

1½ ounces	Herradura tequila
2½ ounces	grapefruit juice
2½ ounces	Squirt
garnish	lime wedge

Combine all the ingredients in a shaker with ice.

Shake for 10 seconds and strain into a salt-rimmed glass.

Garnish with a lime wedge.

TACO MILAGRO
SHRIMP TAMALES

The concoctions that fill tamales are varied and numerous. They are easy to eat without utensils and almost everyone loves them. They also freeze amazingly well and make a great holiday gift. These shrimp tamales from culinary whiz Robert Del Grande are clean and fresh tasting - an elegant spin on a versatile dish.

YIELD: 12 SMALL TAMALES

12	shrimp, large, shell-on, deveined	½ cup	Monterey Jack cheese, mild, grated
2¼ teaspoons	salt	1	jalapeño or serrano, thinly sliced
6 cups	water	½ cup	crème fraiche or sour cream
½ cup	coarse white grits (not instant)	for garnish	lime wedges
½ cup	masa harina		cilantro sprigs
3 tablespoons	butter, unsalted		
12	corn husks, dried, soaked in water until flexible		

Place the shrimp in a pot and cover with 4 cups of room temperature water and 1½ teaspoons of the salt. Bring the water to a boil and then turn off the heat. Let the shrimp cook for 1 minute, then drain. Remove the shells and cut the shrimp into small pieces. Set aside.

For the tamale dough, combine the remaining water and salt in a sauce pot and bring to a boil. Combine the grits and masa harina. While stirring, slowly add the grits mixture. Lower the heat and cook covered, stirring occasionally, until the mixture is very, very thick, about 20 to 30 minutes. Remove from the heat and stir in the butter until completely incorporated. Allow the dough to cool to room temperature.

To assemble the tamales, lay out the corn husks on a work surface, making sure to dry them. Place 2 spoonfuls of the tamale dough on a corn husk and smooth to a ¼-inch thick rectangle. Add some of the grated cheese and chopped shrimp. Place a thin slice of jalapeño over the shrimp and cheese. Fold up the corn husk to form a tamale. Fold up the bottom and tie in place with either a strip of corn husk or string. Repeat the process until all of the dough is used. Refrigerate for a minimum of 1 hour.

Cook the tamales in a large steamer until heated through and firm to the touch, about 15 minutes.

Serve the tamales with the crème fraiche or sour cream, cilantro leaves and lime wedges. A favorite bottled hot sauce is also nice.

SANGRITA

Sangrita, meaning "little blood", is most often accompanied by a shot of tequila. It is thought to be a palate cleanser and also a digestive aid.

YIELD: 8 SERVINGS

1 cup	bloody mary mix, spicy
1 cup	orange juice, fresh

Combine the bloody mary mix and orange juice. Refrigerate.

Serve alongside a salt-rimmed shot glass of your favorite tequila and a lime wedge.

SABORES

SOPESITOS ESPECIALES

Antojito literally translates to 'small craving'. But, trust me, your craving for these beautiful little appetizers will be grande. A sope is a small thick tortilla with a pinched lip on the edge that corrals the delicious topping of potato, carrot, chorizo and crumbled queso fresco. The guajillo chile salsa that is added to the masa when forming the tortillas, is a beautiful orange-red and gives the sopes a bright, subtly spicy flavor. It tastes amazing on just about everything. Double the batch called for here and keep some in the fridge for tacos, tamales, and more.

YIELD: 20 SOPESITOS

GUAJILLO CHILE SALSA

12	guajillo chiles		1 cup	water
¼ teaspoon	cumin, whole		to taste	salt
1	garlic clove			

Seed, devein and tear the guajillo chiles into pieces. Place all the ingredients in a blender and liquefy. Strain to remove skins and any remaining seeds. Add salt to taste.

TOPPING

5	white potatoes, large (not russet)		2 tablespoons	oil
1	carrot, large		½ cup	chorizo
			1 teaspoon	salt

Peel the potatoes and carrot. Boil until cooked but still slightly firm. Medium-dice the potatoes and carrots. In a Teflon pan, heat oil. Add the chorizo and sauté. Add the diced potatoes and carrot. Add the salt and adjust to taste. Don't overstir. Set aside and keep warm.

SOPES

2 cups	Maseca		2 cups	water
½ teaspoon	salt		for frying	oil
½ cup	guajillo chile salsa*		for garnish	queso fresco

In a large mixing bowl, combine the Maseca with the salt, salsa, and 1 to 1½ cups of water. Knead the mixture. Add more water if the mixture is too dry.

Warm a dry griddle or skillet on medium-high heat. Break the dough into 20 equal-sized balls. Place each ball between 2 sheets of plastic or wax paper (a Ziploc bag with the zipper cut off and split down the sides works well) and smash down with your hand or with a small square cutting board. You're forming small, thick, round tortillas. Keep the tortillas moist by covering with a wet towel.

Place the tortillas onto a griddle or skillet. Flip after about 45 seconds, then remove from the heat after 30 seconds. They will not be cooked through. Quickly pinch up the edges to form a brim, about ¼-inch high, before they cool. With a fork, pierce the top of the tortillas 3 to 4 times. Go on to the next batch until all 20 have been formed.

To assemble, heat about 1-inch of oil in a skillet, over high heat. Fry the sopes until golden, about 4 to 5 minutes, flipping them halfway through. Drain on paper towels.

Place a spoonful of the topping on each sope. Top with crumbled queso fresco, they recommend "La Vaquita".

AGUA DE MELÓN

1	cantaloupe, medium, ripe
1 gallon	water
1½ cups	sugar

Peel the cantaloupe and cut into medium-sized cubes. Add to the blender along with ¼ cup of water. Purée, adding more water as necessary to keep things moving. If you're not a fan of pulp, pour through a strainer into a garrafón or large pitcher. Add 1 cup of sugar and the remaining water and stir well. Taste and add an additional ½ cup of sugar as needed. Serve over ice.

You can substitute granulated Splenda for the sugar.

LA GUADALUPANA
POBLANO MOLE ENCHILADAS

The state of Puebla claims to be the birthplace of mole sauce and offers up a legendary explanation of its roots. During the colonial era, the nuns of the Convent of Santa Rosa were expected to receive the archbishop, which sent them into a panic as they were very poor and had little to feed him. The nuns prayed and eventually pulled together the ingredients they did have - chiles, spices, nuts, seeds and a little chocolate. Served over turkey meat, the archbishop is said to have loved it.

YIELD: 15 TO 20 SERVINGS

POBLANO MOLE

3 ounces	pasilla chiles	⅓ cup	raisins
2 ounces	mulato chiles	¼ cup	sesame seeds, roasted
2 ounces	guajillo chiles	1 tablespoon	chile seeds, reserved
2 ounces	ancho chiles	1	3.3-ounce Mexican chocolate tablet, cut into pieces
1 ounce	chipotle chiles		
2 tablespoons	olive oil		
½	white onion, chopped	1	corn tortilla, toasted & broken into pieces
2	garlic cloves		
¼ teaspoon	black pepper	½	bolillo bread roll, brushed with salted butter & toasted, broken into pieces
⅓ cup	almonds, roasted		
⅓ cup	peanuts, roasted		
¼ cup	pumpkin seeds, roasted	4 cups	chicken broth

Preheat the oven to 300˚F.

Wearing latex or vinyl gloves, remove the stems, seeds and membranes from the chiles. Reserve 1 tablespoon of the chile seeds. Place all the chiles on a sheet pan and bake for 3 minutes. Remove from oven. Put the chiles in a bowl and cover with boiling water. Soak for a minimum of 1 hour.

In a dutch oven or large stockpot, heat the olive oil over medium heat. Add the onion, garlic, and black pepper and cook for 3 to 5 minutes, stirring constantly, until they release their aroma. Stir in the almonds, peanuts, pumpkin seeds, raisins, sesame seeds and reserved chile seeds. Cook for 2 to 3 minutes. Add the chocolate, tortilla and bread and stir to combine. Remove from heat. Place the mixture in a blender or food processor and puree in 3 batches, adding ⅓ cup of broth to each batch. Strain the mixture.

Drain the chiles but reserve the water. Puree the chiles in 3 batches, adding about ⅓ cup of the reserved liquid to each batch. Strain the pureed chiles. Heat a little olive oil in a dutch oven over medium heat, add the pureed chiles and cook for about 3 minutes. Next, add the seed and nut mixture, stir to combine and cook for 3 to 5 minutes. Cool and refrigerate the paste.

When ready to eat, heat ½ cup chicken broth in a saucepan over high heat. Add ½ cup mole paste and be sure to whisk, constantly, to combine. Add more chicken stock and/or paste until the desired consistency is reached. To serve with enchiladas, roll roasted shredded chicken in warmed tortillas, top with the mole sauce, avocado slices, queso fresco and sesame seeds.

This mole can be stored, covered, in the refrigerator for about a month, or you can freeze it for up to a year.

I am not going to lie to you. This recipe is very complex and time-consuming, but it is so traditional that a Mexican cookbook without a mole recipe would have been a crime. You will have a great sense of accomplishment if you even attempt it. And, if you think you've failed, remember this: Mole is like a pot of beans. It gets better the longer it sits. The flavor will continue to develop, so it will taste different on day one than on day three. A little bitterness is easily counteracted with the addition of some salt (yes, salt). A little sugar never hurts either.

If mole's not your thing, you're not alone. But, if it is, then this is the place for it. In addition to mole, Chef Trancito Diaz never disappoints with his spicy verde chicken enchiladas, the chorizo and potato-filled breakfast torta, cinnamon-roasted coffee, pastries and his amazing tres leches cake. If you're lucky, he might even sneak a shot of Bailey's in your cup of cinnamon coffee. Nice!

Sylvia's opened in 1998 and became so famous for the enchiladas they serve that the restaurant was renamed Sylvia's Enchilada Kitchen. Owner and Chef Sylvia Casares continues to create unique enchilada recipes that reflect some of the most popular varieties served throughout Mexico and Texas. She has since opened a second location and is now also recognized for her mesquite-grilled meats like cabrito, shrimp, carne asada and quail.

SALSA ROJA

13	cascabel chiles (stems & seeds removed)
4	arbol chiles (stems removed)
2 cups	water
2 tablespoons	vegetable oil
½	onion, medium, diced
2	garlic cloves, minced
1¾ teaspoons	salt
1¼ cups	water

Combine the chiles and water in a medium saucepan. Bring to a boil and simmer for 15 minutes. Allow to cool for about 10 minutes.

Blend the chiles on high for about 1 minute. Strain the puréed chiles to remove the skins that did not liquefy.

Using a medium skillet, heat the vegetable oil and sauté the onion and garlic for 3 to 5 minutes. Add the puréed chiles, salt and remaining water. Simmer for about 5 minutes. Set aside.

SYLVIA'S ENCHILADA KITCHEN
MORELIA ENCHILADAS

A fresh and colorful garnish of radishes, thinly sliced romaine lettuce and red onion combine beautifully with crumbly white cheese and Sylvia's famous red chile Salsa Roja. Sylvia will tell you that this recipe is reminiscent of the enchiladas served in homes all over Mexico. Very authentic, very earthy and beyond delicious.

YIELD: 12 ENCHILADAS

12 (6-inch)	corn tortillas		salsa roja*
	spicing sauce*	for garnish	radish, thinly sliced
1 tablespoon	vegetable oil		red onion, thinly sliced
1 pound	queso fresco, grated (reserve ⅓ cup for garnish)		romaine or iceberg lettuce, thinly sliced
1	onion, medium, diced		queso fresco, grated

Preheat the oven to 350˚F.

Dip the tortillas in the spicing sauce 1 by 1 and set side.

Heat the oil in a medium skillet over medium-high heat. Place 1 tortilla at a time in the hot oil and using a spatula, turn over quickly. Total time in the oil should be about 30 seconds. Remove the tortilla and place on a plate. Repeat with remaining tortillas.

Place about 2 tablespoons of queso fresco and a little onion down the center of each tortilla. Roll the tortilla into an enchilada and place in a casserole dish, seam side down. Repeat until all tortillas are filled.

Pour the salsa roja over the enchiladas and bake for about 5 to 7 minutes.

Garnish with radish, red onion, lettuce and queso fresco.

SPICING SAUCE

7	cascabel or guajillo chiles (stems & seeds removed)	1¾ cups	water
3	chiles de arbol (stems removed)	1 cup	vegetable oil

Combine both chiles and water in a small saucepan. Bring to a boil, reduce heat and then simmer for 15 minutes.

Allow to cool for about 10 to 15 minutes. Strain the puréed chiles to remove the skins that did not liquefy.

CYCLONE ANAYA'S
LOBSTER ENCHILADAS

This decadent dish is truly the best thing I have ever had in my mouth. The rich Chardonnay cream sauce and the garlicky lobster make for perfectly luxurious enchiladas!

YIELD: 12 ENCHILADAS

6 tablespoons	butter, unsalted	2¼ cups	white Mexican cheese, grated
2¼ pounds	lobster meat, chopped	3	green onions, finely chopped
6	garlic cloves, minced		
pinch	kosher salt	3 teaspoons	pine nuts, toasted
2¼ cups	Chardonnay sauce*	¾ cup	Cojita cheese, grated
12 (8-inch)	flour tortillas		

Heat the butter in a large skillet over medium heat. Add the lobster meat, garlic and a pinch of salt. Cook for 4 minutes. Add ½ cup of the Chardonnay cream sauce and mix together. Remove from the heat.

Preheat your oven broiler. Quickly, warm the tortillas on a flat grill and set aside.

Spread ¼ cup of the filling down the middle of each tortilla. Roll and place seam side down in a 9-by 13-inch dish. Cover the tortillas with the Chardonnay cream sauce and sprinkle with the Mexican white cheese.

Place the dish under the broiler until the cheese melts.

Sprinkle the green onions and pine nuts on top of the enchiladas, then sprinkle with the Cojita cheese.

CHARDONNAY SAUCE

4 tablespoons	butter, unsalted	2 tablespoons	water
2	garlic cloves, minced	4 cups	heavy cream
1	yellow onion, diced	1 teaspoon	salt
2 cups	Chardonnay wine		
2 tablespoons	corn starch		

Melt the butter in a saucepan over medium heat. Add the garlic and onions and cook until lightly browned, about 10 minutes.

Add the wine and simmer for about 5 to 10 minutes, or until the wine is reduced by half.

In a small bowl, combine the corn starch and water, mixing well. Set aside.

Next, add the heavy cream and bring to a boil. Reduce heat to a simmer, add the corn starch mixture and stir really well.

Continue to cook over medium heat, stirring constantly, until the sauce begins to thicken. Let simmer over very low heat for 5 minutes. Remove from heat.

Cyclone Anaya's was founded in 1966 by Mexican and U.S. champion wrestler Cyclone Anaya and his wife, Carolina. After his retirement from wrestling, they compiled the best of his wife's amazing homemade recipes and opened the legendary addition to Houston's culinary scene. They have been going strong and pleasing diners for some forty years.

SKINNY MARGARITA

YIELD: 1 SERVING

1½ ounces	Patron silver
1 ounce	Patron Citronage
1½ ounces	lime juice, fresh
1 ounce	agave nectar

Combine all the ingredients. Shake with ice and pour into a salt-rimmed martini glass.

Berryhill tamales are drenched in tradition. Walter Berryhill began with a pushcart in 1928 and sold his incredible homemade tamales on the street corners of the upscale River Oaks neighborhood until he retired in 1960. For the next 30 years, his tamale recipe and antique cart would sit in a warehouse until being rediscovered by an entrepreneur who used those recipes to open Berryhill Tamales and Tacos in 1993.

In 1997, The Anon Group purchased the company and boosted the eatery from a "Mom & Pop" establishment to a restaurant company now called Berryhill Baja Grill. They have expanded and still use Walter's signature recipes to serve five varieties - beef, chicken, pork, bean and the famed spinach and corn - all handmade and steamed in the husk.

BERRYHILL BAJA GRILL
VERDE CHICKEN ENCHILADAS

Tomatillos are the key ingredient to this dish. They may look a little foreign at first, but once you remove the paper-like husk, you will find them to be very similar to a standard small green tomato. When shopping, keep in mind that the freshness and greenness of the husk are quality criteria and they should be firm and bright green.

YIELD: 24 ENCHILADAS

TOMATILLO SAUCE

2 pounds	tomatillos	2½ tablespoons	garlic, peeled, finely chopped
½ pound	jalapeños, halved	¾ bunch	cilantro, chopped
1 tablespoon	olive oil	1½ tablespoons	chicken base
½ pound	white onion, chopped	½ cup	water

Husk and wash the tomatillos. Boil the tomatillos and jalapeños in just enough water to cover, for 45 minutes or until translucent and mushy. Drain the water and reserve. Using a blender or an immersion blender, process the mixture until smooth. Add the onion, garlic and cilantro to the oil in a large stockpot. Cook on medium heat for a few minutes.

Add the pureed mixture, chicken base, water and the reserved cooking water to the stockpot. Simmer for 2 to 3 hours.

CHICKEN MIXTURE

2½ pounds	chicken breast, cooked & chopped	½ cup	tomatillo sauce*
1 cup	Monterey Jack cheese, shredded		

In a bowl, combine the chicken, cheese and the tomatillo sauce. Set aside.

ASSEMBLY

1 tablespoon	vegetable oil	3 cups	tomatillo sauce
12 (6-inch)	corn tortillas, white	1½ cups	Monterey Jack cheese
4 cups	chicken mixture		

Preheat the oven to 350˚F.

Heat the oil in a skillet over medium-high heat and add the tortillas, for just a minute or so per side. Scoop ⅓ cup of the chicken mixture onto a tortilla and roll up, seam side down in a casserole dish. Repeat with the remaining tortillas. Cover with the sauce and the cheese.

Cover the casserole dish with aluminum foil. Bake for 10 minutes or until the cheese is melted.

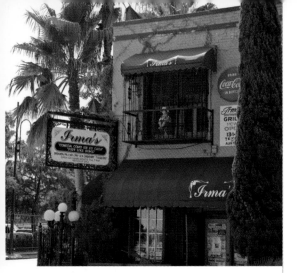

IRMA'S FAMOUS LEMONADE

3 cups	watermelon
1 cup	pineapple
1 cup	strawberries
1 cup	cantaloupe
1 cup	green or red grapes
¾ cup	orange juice, fresh
½ to 1 cup	Mexican lime or lemon juice
½ to 1 cup	sugar

Cut the fruit into bite-sized pieces then blend each separately with an equal amount of water. Strain the pineapple, cantaloupe, and grape juices.

Add the orange and lime or lemon juices. Dissolve the sugar in a little hot water and add to the juice. Garnish with cut fruit, in the glass and on the rim.

IRMA'S
CHILE RELLENO

Irma Galvan is a super-star celebrity chef in Houston, who is said to be loved more than the Astros. Bobby Flay presented this sweetheart of a lady the prestigious James Beard Award in 2008. She's got it going on!

YIELD: 6 SERVINGS

FILLING

6	poblano peppers	½ teaspoon	salt
1 tablespoon	olive oil	¼ teaspoon	cumin
1 pound	lean ground round	½ teaspoon	black pepper, ground
½ cup	onion, chopped	for garnish	queso fresco, crumbled
1	garlic clove, minced		cilantro, chopped
1 cup	tomatoes, diced		

Roast the poblanos over a gas flame or under the oven broiler, turning until blistered and slightly charred all over. Put the peppers into a heavy plastic bag and set aside to steam for 10 to 20 minutes. Peel the skin off the poblanos. Carefully make a lengthwise slit in each of the peppers and remove the seeds and membranes. Rinse and drain well. Use paper towels to pat the peppers dry.

To prepare the stuffing, first heat the oil in a large skillet or saucepan, add the meat and brown. Add the chopped onion and garlic, stirring for 1 minute. Next, add the tomatoes, salt, cumin and black pepper and cook for about 10 to 15 minutes. Stir constantly until meat is somewhat dry. Set aside to cool. When cool, fill the peppers with the stuffing but leave enough room to overlap the slit edges. Place the peppers on a sheet pan, cover with foil or saran wrap and put in the freezer for a minimum of 20 minutes.

BATTER FOR CHILES

4	eggs, room temperature	3 cups	cooking oil
1 cup	flour		

In a bowl, separate the eggs. Beat the egg whites until stiff and foamy. Add the egg yolks to the whites and blend. Put the flour in a separate bowl and set aside.

Add about 3 cups of oil to a deep skillet and heat to 350˚F. Flour dust then batter the peppers and carefully drop into the hot oil. Fry to a golden brown on all sides. Remove from the oil and place on paper towels to absorb excess grease. To serve, top the chile rellenos with ranchero sauce and garnish with queso fresco and chopped cilantro.

SALSA RANCHERA

⅓ cup	cooking oil	4	tomatoes, medium, chopped
1	onion, large, chopped		
1	garlic clove, minced	1 (14 oz.) can	tomatoes, chopped
2	red bell peppers, chopped	dash	cumin, ground

In a skillet, heat the cooking oil until hot. Brown the onion, garlic, peppers and tomatoes for 2 minutes. Add the can of tomatoes and simmer for 10 to 15 minutes.

EL TIEMPO
Carne Asada

Inspired from the famous "Tampiquena" known throughout Mexico, El Tiempo has served a version of this dish for over thirty years. It is one of those dishes that is deeply rooted in their heritage and makes its way onto every re-print of their menus. It's part of the family!

Succulent tenderloin filet is seasoned with a special spice mix, basted with their prized black sauce and cooked over an open, mesquite wood burning grill - then placed on a bed of caramelized onions, served with lime wedges and grilled jalapenos... it almost melts in your mouth.

YIELD: 8 SERVINGS

TENDERLOIN

3 to 4 pounds	beef tenderloin

BLACK SAUCE

¼ cup	water		½ tablespoon	A-1
1 tablespoon	extra virgin olive oil		⅓ cup	V-8
6 tablespoons	Maggi sauce*		¼ tablespoon	spice mix*
¼ tablespoon	bbq sauce			

Combine all ingredients in a blender. Blend until emulsified.

SPICE MIX

¼ cup	black pepper		1⅓ tablespoons	Lawry's or seasoned salt
¼ cup	garlic, granulated		1 tablespoon	kosher salt
1 tablespoon	cumin, ground			

Mix all ingredients in a small bowl or shaker.

To prepare the tenderloin for this dish, approach your first cut as if cutting the meat to serve it, across the grain, cutting the tenderloin into 'rolls' about 4-inches wide. Using your left palm to press down on each roll, take the knife into your right hand and begin to cut into the roll on the right side, ½-inch from the cutting board. Use your left hand to roll the meat towards your left as you butterfly it open with your right hand. Be careful to keep your blade parallel to the cutting board and maintain the ½-inch-thick cut. Your goal here is to produce a cut of meat that mimics a flank or skirt steak - ½-inch-thick, 4-inches wide and 8-to 12-inches long. A narrow, slender knife works best, as a larger chef's knife will obstruct your view while cutting. Season both sides of the meat with the spice mix.

Place the meat on a hot grill to get a good sear on each side. Move to the cooler part of the grill and baste both sides of the meat. Continue to baste the meat, until temperature registers 135°F. Be careful not to over cook. Let the meat rest for 10 minutes before cutting.

Recipe Note: You may substitute equal parts of soy sauce and worchestershire for Maggi sauce.

BORRACHO BEANS

YIELD: 4 TO 5 CUPS

5 cups	water
2 cups	pinto beans
1	bay leaf
¾ teaspoon	oregano
1 tablespoon	garlic, fresh
½ teaspoon	cumin, ground
1 tablespoon	salt
3 slices	bacon, chopped
¼ pound	chorizo
¼ pound	ham, diced
2 cups	tomato, diced
2 cups	onion, diced
2 tablespoons	jalapeño, finely diced
1	beer
2 tablespoons	cilantro, chopped

Add the water, beans, bay leaf, oregano, garlic, cumin and salt to a stockpot. Bring to a boil, then simmer for 2 hours or until tender.

In a separate pan, fry the bacon until crisp, then add the chorizo and ham. Drain off some of the grease. Add the tomato, onion and jalapeño and continue to cook for about 5 minutes.

Add the mixture to the beans along with the beer. Let the beans simmer for 15 minutes more and up to 2 hours, as you want all the flavors to meld.

Add the cilantro at the very end of the cooking process.

LA VIDA LOCAL

YIELD: 1 SERVING

1¼ ounces	Dulce Vida Reposado tequila
¼ ounce	St. Germaine Elder Flower liqueur
1 ounce	jamaica infused syrup*
1 ounce	lime juice, fresh

Combine all ingredients in a shaker. Shake for 10 seconds. Pour into a salt-rimmed glass.

JAMAICA INFUSED SYRUP

1 cup	water
¾ cup	agave nectar
15	jamaica (hibiscus) flowers

Combine in a saucepan and heat to just below boiling. Remove from heat, cover to steep for 15 minutes. Then strain and refrigerate.

HAVEN
PORK BELLY AL PASTOR TORTA

This gourmet torta is both spicy and sweet, hot and cool. The roasted corn on the cob is topped with tangy crema fresca and lime, making it a perfect summertime side. Crema fresca may be found at the supermarket or you can make your own by adding a little lime juice to sour cream or even Greek yogurt. I recently read somewhere that pork belly is the 'catnip' of foodies. If pork belly is not your thing, don't despair. Pork tenderloin is a wonderful substitution, as is pork shoulder or butt.

YIELD: 8 SERVINGS

6	guajillo chiles	1 to 2 teaspoons	adobo sauce (from canned chipotles)
1	white onion, large	2½ to 3 pounds	pork belly
1	pineapple, peeled, cut into ½-inch thick rounds	8	torta rolls
½ cup	orange juice, fresh	¼ cup	cilantro, fresh, chopped
¼ cup	white vinegar, distilled	½ cup	tomato, diced
3	garlic cloves, halved	½ cup	lettuce, shredded
2 teaspoons	kosher salt, coarse	1	avocado
1 teaspoon	Mexican oregano, dried	for garnish	crema fresca
1 teaspoon	cumin, ground		salsa verde
2	chipotle chiles, (canned), small		lime wedges

Preheat oven to 350°F. Place the guajillo chiles on a baking pan and heat in the oven until puffed up and aromatic, about 3 minutes. Remove from the oven and allow to cool. Remove the seeds and membranes, tear into pieces and process to a fine powder in a spice or coffee grinder.

Coarsely chop 1 half of the onion. Coarsely chop 2 pineapple rounds, cover and chill the remaining pineapple. Place the chopped onion and chopped pineapple in a blender. Add the orange juice, vinegar, chile powder, garlic, salt, oregano, cumin, chipotles and adobo sauce. Purée the marinade until smooth. Place the pork in a large resealable plastic bag. Add the marinade and seal the bag, releasing excess air. Turn to coat. Chill at least 4 hours and up to 1 day.

Preheat the oven to 300°F. Remove the pork from the bag and place on a wire rack, skin side up, in a roasting pan. Place the reserved pineapple rounds on the pork. Cover with foil and roast for 5 to 6 hours or until the pork is tender.

Sear the pork on a plancha or in an iron skillet on both sides over high heat until crispy. Dice the pineapple rings and place in a mixing bowl. Thinly slice the pork and combine with the pineapple.

Finely chop the remaining onion half and place in a medium bowl. Add the cilantro and toss to combine. Fill the torta rolls with the pork mixture, the cilantro and onion mixture, lettuce, avocado and crema fresca. Serve with salsa verde and lime wedges.

SANTOS - THE TASTE OF MEXICO
CARNITAS

These sweet little morsels' unique taste comes from just a hint of clove and cinnamon. A traditional dish, with roots in the Jalisco region of Mexico, Carnitas are a very versatile item that can be incorporated into other recipes. From cream cheese carnita tamales to stuffing for chile rellenos, you'll have a basic foundation from which you can create many amazing dishes. If you like your food spicy, add a couple of fresh jalapeños or serranos to the pot.

YIELD: 4 TO 6 SERVINGS

3 pounds	pork shoulder or butt, boneless	pinch	cloves, ground
1 tablespoon	salt	1 stick	cinnamon
1 tablespoon	black pepper, ground	½ cup	whole milk
1 tablespoon	garlic powder	½ cup	Coca-Cola
8 cups	water	for frying	olive oil

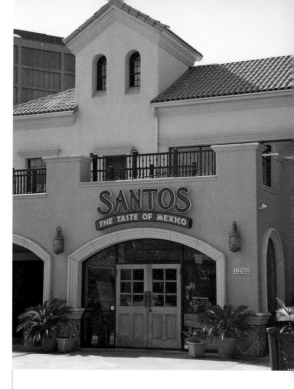

Remove most of the visible fat and cut the pork into 5 to 6 pieces.

Season the pork generously with salt, pepper and garlic powder. Add the pork to a large stock pot and cover with the water.

Add a pinch of powdered cloves and a pinch of cinnamon or a cinnamon stick. If using a cinnamon stick, be sure to remove it after 20 minutes or it will overpower the dish. Let cook over medium heat for 1 hour and 30 minutes.

Next, add the milk and Coca-Cola to the pot and continue to cook for another 20 to 30 minutes.

Remove the meat from the pot and allow to cool. When cool, cut into smaller 2 to 3-inch cubes.

Heat the olive oil in a large dutch oven or deep skillet over medium-high heat. Add the cubes of pork, in small batches and cook for just a few minutes until they get a little crispy.

Serve with charro beans, rice, tomatillo salsa, sour cream, chopped cilantro, lime wedges and plenty of tortillas.

Santos - The Taste of Mexico is a fairly new Houston restaurant, but it's already a favorite. Located on Houston's west side, the upscale casual eatery features soft lighting, charming interiors, an amazing bar and a very diverse menu. Even foodies with sophisticated palates will appreciate the offerings of seafood and traditional Mexican fare. And, if being indecisive is an issue when ordering, you can always try the Grande Santos Villa Del Carmen platter which features lobster, shrimp, chicken, quail, sausage and ribs. Regulars there claim to be so spoiled by the food, they can't bring themselves to eat anywhere else.

HORCHATA

2 cups	rice, long grain, parboiled
4 cups	hot water
2	cinnamon sticks
6	almonds
1	lemon zest
1 tablespoon	vanilla
6 tablespoons	sweetened condensed milk

Soak the rice and cinnamon sticks in a large pot of water. Let sit overnight.

The next day, blend the rice, cinnamon and water. Add the other ingredients, and blend well. Strain through a cheesecloth. Serve mixture over ice.

DONERAKI
CHIPOTLE CHICKEN

The brainchild of Cesar Rodriguez - Doneraki Bar & Grill is a booming restaurant with three locations, an impressive feat for a man who started with just six hundred borrowed dollars in 1973. Boasting staff members that have served there for thirty-seven years, their moles, tortillas and marinated Tacos de Trompo are among the favorites, as is the impressive Sunday brunch.

This dish is a favorite at Doneraki, of customers and staff alike. It's also a surefire hit with chipotle lovers but anyone can enjoy it as it isn't too spicy. Be mindful to incorporate those final ingredients quickly and then get the mixture off of the heat - lest the butter and wine separate.

YIELD: 6 SERVINGS

CHICKEN

6 (6 oz.)	chicken breasts	to taste	salt & pepper

Season and grill the chicken breasts until done.

SAUCE

½ cup	butter, unsalted	½ teaspoon	black pepper
¼ cup	sherry wine	1 tablespoon	adobo sauce (from canned chipotles)
1 tablespoon	soy sauce		
½ teaspoon	garlic powder		

Heat the sherry in a saucepan. After the alcohol has evaporated, add the butter until melted. Add the rest of the ingredients and continue to stir.

Do not simmer. Pull off of the heat after adding the ingredients.

SPINACH

1 bunch	spinach	¼ cup	mushrooms, sliced
¼ cup	olive oil	to taste	salt & pepper
1 tablespoon	onion	18 slices	queso fresco
1 tablespoon	garlic, minced		

Preheat the oven to 350˚F.

Wash and clean the spinach. Add the olive oil, onions, garlic, and mushrooms and sauté over medium heat. Add the spinach and salt and pepper to taste.

Place the chicken breasts on a sheet pan or oven-proof plate. Brush a little of the chipotle sauce on each breast and top with just enough spinach to cover.

Add 3 rectangular pieces of cheese on top of the spinach. Heat in oven for about 5 minutes or until the cheese slightly melts.

Remove from the oven and spoon a little more sauce over each breast.

GRINGO'S MEXICAN KITCHEN
CARNE GUISADA

Carne guisada is a hearty and homey Mexican beef stew. Gringo's carne guisada is my favorite for many reasons. Not only is it flavorful and super tender, it's also super lean. They take special care to trim all visible fat from their meat. For the best results, be sure to take your time when cutting the cubes of beef and dicing the vegetables. Consistency is the key here - 1-inch cubes for beef and ½-inch dice for vegetables. In fact, there's never been a better time to befriend your butcher. Ask nicely and he just might trim and cube the meat for you! Also, keep the lid on while simmering so the ingredients continue to soak up their own juices during cooking. If you tend to like things a little spicier, consider using a can of Rotel tomatoes with habañeros in place of the crushed tomatoes.

YIELD: 6 TO 8 SERVINGS

3½ pounds	top sirloin	1½ cups	yellow onions
3½ teaspoons	salt	1½ cups	green bell peppers
½ tablespoon	black pepper, fine	1 (14.5 oz.) can	tomatoes, crushed
1 tablespoon	cumin, ground		
2¼ teaspoons	garlic powder		

Clean and trim most of the visible fat from the meat. Cut the meat into 1-inch cubes.

Season the beef with the salt, pepper, cumin and garlic powder. Cut the onions and peppers into ½-inch dice and set aside.

Put the meat into a dutch oven or large stock pot and cover. Don't be scared, the meat will release the necessary oils so that added liquid should not be necessary. Cook on medium-high heat for 15 minutes. Reduce the heat to medium and continue cooking, covered, for 40 minutes.

Add the onions and peppers to the beef cubes and mix thoroughly. Continue to cook, covered, on medium heat for 20 minutes.

Next, pour in the crushed tomatoes and blend thoroughly.

Continue to simmer, covered, on medium heat for 20 more minutes.

Test the meat for tenderness. If it pulls apart easily - it's done! If it does not pull apart easily and remains tough, reduce the heat to low and cook, covered, in 10 minute intervals, until the beef is tender.

If the gravy is too thin for your liking, add a pinch of flour (diluted in ½ cup water) to thicken.

Serve with rice, beans and tortillas - and awesome with guacamole!

Recipe Note: We used to serve a dish called Tortilla Relleno at my restaurant- carne guisada rolled in a flour tortilla, burrito-style, topped with salsa roja and cheese...it was hard-to-beat!

Gringo's Mexican Kitchen owner Russell Ybarra was reared in the restaurant business. Ybarra's parents opened El Toro Mexican Restaurant in 1960 and the entire family learned the restaurant trade as it grew. Many of Gringo's recipes are inspired by El Toro and their continued commitment to provide amazing food with quality ingredients.

This always-packed eatery offers classic fare like homemade salsa, tortillas and fajitas, but ordering the more inventive dishes like Chicken Marisco - a chicken breast smothered in their signature white wine cheese sauce with sautéed shrimp and crawfish tails - will leave you feeling especially satisfied.

Alex Sneider, co-owner of Las Ventanas Restaurant and Cantina comes from a family of established restaurant owners. He practically grew up in the kitchen of his father's beloved Las Alamedas eatery and eventually managed there for 15 years before deciding to open a similar concept of his own - Las Ventanas Restaurant and Cantina. He offers amazing authentic Mexican cuisine in the tradition of Las Alamedas - flavorful, fresh food with a singular secret ingredient - passion.

LAS VENTANAS
HUACHINANGO VERACRUZANA

This dish truly exemplifies the authentic flavors of the Veracuz region of Mexico. The appreciation for the spanish olive in the southeast coastal area really shines through. Red snapper is the preferred fish for this recipe, but you can swap it out for virtually any whitefish. Cut the recipe in half to make an amazing dinner for two.

YIELD: 6 SERVINGS

VERACRUZANA SAUCE

6 pounds	tomatoes	¾ cup	green olives
1 pound	onions	¾ cup	white wine
2	green bell peppers	4 cups	chicken stock
¾ cup	garlic	2 tablespoons	chicken bouillon
2 tablespoons	olive oil	2	bay leaves
1 tablespoon	basil	1 tablespoon	capers
2 tablespoons	parsley		

Slice the tomatoes and then cut the tomatoes into julienne strips.

Cut the onion and green bell pepper into julienne strips. Chop the garlic.

Heat the olive oil in a saucepan, over medium heat, and add the onions, peppers, and garlic. Cook for about 5 minutes.

Chop the basil and parsley. Slice the olives. Then, add the basil, parsley, wine, chicken stock, chicken bouillon, bay leaves, green olives and capers.

Finally, add the tomatoes and cook for 6 to 10 minutes over medium heat.

FISH

6	snapper fillets	2 tablespoons	olive oil
1 cup	Italian dressing		

Preheat the oven to 350˚F.

Marinate the fish in the Italian dressing for about 15 to 30 minutes. Heat the oil in a sauté pan over medium-high heat. Add the fish and cook for about 3 minutes per side.

Place the fish into a 9-by-13-inch casserole dish. Spoon the tomato sauce over the filets. Bake for 10 to 15 minutes, or until the fish flakes easily with a fork.

Serve the leftover sauce on the side.

LUPE TORTILLA
CHIPOTLE COSTILLAS

If you want to be the hero at your next barbecue, make these heavenly, smoky, pork ribs. This foolproof recipe yields ribs that literally fall off of the bone. They are then slathered in a rich, delicious chipotle sauce and drizzled with honey.

YIELD: 6 TO 10 SERVINGS

RIBS

2 to 4 racks	baby back ribs

RIB RUB

2 tablespoons	chili powder	1 tablespoon	Italian herb blend (w/o rosemary)
2 tablespoons	garlic, granulated		
2 tablespoons	salt	¼ teaspoon	cumin, ground
1 tablespoon	black pepper		

Combine all ingredients in a small bowl or shaker. Reserve 1 tablespoon for the sauce recipe below.

SAUCE

6 tablespoons	chipotles (canned), in abobo sauce	1 cup	water
4 cups	bbq sauce	1 tablespoon	rib rub*
1 cup	jalapeño juice	to taste	honey
1 cup	tomato purée		

Preheat the oven to 350˚F.

Thoroughly coat both sides of the ribs with the rub (be sure to leave 1 tablespoon for the sauce) and wrap in aluminum foil.

Place in the oven and roast for 2 hours.

Remove from the oven and allow to completely cool. Then, cut the ribs apart.

To make the sauce, combine all of the ingredients (except the honey) into a blender and purée until smooth.

Toss the ribs in the sauce and place them on a hot grill for about 4 to 6 minutes per side.

Remove from the grill and lightly drizzle with honey to glaze.

Lupe Tortilla was founded in 1983 by Stan and Audrey Holt. Their sons, Peter and Judson, are both Culinary Institute of America graduates and continue their legacy.

They boast eight Houston locations and plans are underway for three more Houston eateries plus locations in Austin and San Antonio.

They are famous for grilled items like fajitas, Chicken Lupe, fish tacos and, of course, these ribs. They also pride themselves on the hand-rolled, ultra-thin 12-inch tortillas for which the restaurant is named.

Chuy's was founded in 1982 in Austin, Texas and serves authentic and affordable Mexican cuisine in a funky atmosphere. They boast twenty-three locations in Texas, two in Tennessee, one in Alabama and one in Kentucky. Every love-filled plate is served fresh and made-to-order. Known for exceptional service and unbelievable portions, the food here is also a steal. Only one item on the entire menu costs over ten dollars.

One company motto is "If you've seen one Chuy's... you've seen one Chuy's." Each location features very unique decor, an established tradition that began when owners Mike Young and John Zapp had but twenty dollars for their decor budget. Mike used that money to purchase two velvet paintings - one of Stevie Wonder and one of Elvis. Both still hang in the original location.

CHUY'S
STEAK BURRITO

This is, by far, the best burrito I've ever had. I craved it on the way home after just having eaten it. Developed for a green chile festival in the late 90s, the dish was so popular that fans demanded that it be included on the menu. The roasted green chiles (the chain uses nearly 500,000 pounds of Hatch Valley Chiles from New Mexico growers annually) and caramelized onion make it a super fresh and intensely flavored dish that really satisfies.

YIELD: 5 SERVINGS

HATCH GREEN CHILE SAUCE

1 pound	hatch green chiles, roasted	¼ teaspoon	salt
4 tablespoons	beef base	½ pound	onion, diced
1 quart	water	¼ cup	corn starch
¼ teaspoon	black pepper	½ cup	water
¼ teaspoon	garlic salt		

Roast chiles over an open flame or in the oven for 8 to 10 minutes. Remove 85% of the skin and chop. In a large saucepan, dissolve the beef base in the quart of water, over medium-high heat. Add the dry spices and diced onions to the stock and bring mixture to simmer. Allow to simmer long enough for the onions to soften, about 12 minutes. After the onions have softened, add the green chiles. Increase the heat to bring the stock back to a simmer, stirring with a slotted spoon.

In a bowl, combine the water and corn starch and whisk until smooth. With a slotted spoon, slowly stir in the corn starch mixture to the simmering stock. Continue to simmer for an additional 8 to 10 minutes, stirring occasionally, to thicken.

BURRITO ASSEMBLY

5 (12-inch)	flour tortillas	4 cups·	hatch green chile sauce*
2½ pounds	grilled fajita beef	1¼ cups	Monterey Jack cheese

Preheat the oven to 350˚F.

Fill a flour tortilla with ¾ cup grilled fajita beef, 2 tablespoons of chile sauce and 2 tablespoons of Monterey Jack cheese. Fold in sides of the tortilla. Fold in the flap closest to you (bottom). Tuck in both sides with your index fingers. Continue with a rolling motion until the burrito is wrapped with the seam down. Place in a casserole dish. Repeat with remaining tortillas, meat, sauce and cheese. Ladle the remaining sauce over the burritos with an end-to-end motion. Sprinkle the remaining cheese over the top.

Bake for 8 minutes, making sure cheese is melted.

Recipe Note: 1.8 pounds of raw chiles yield about 1 pound of roasted chiles.

THE ORIGINAL NINFA'S
Cochinita Pibil

This dish has roots in the Yucatan region of Mexico. Traditionally made with baby suckling pig wrapped in banana leaves, easily accessible pork shoulder is an excellent substitution. The cool, pickled onions are a nice contrast to the hot, spicy pork. Serve on a fresh banana leaf with fried plantains and crema fresca. To make crema fresca, just add a bit of lime juice to sour cream or Greek yogurt.

YIELD: 8 TO 10 SERVINGS

5 pounds	pork shoulder	3	lemons, juiced
2 tablespoons	salt	1½ cups	pineapple juice
1½ tablespoons	black pepper, ground	½ cup	red wine vinegar
1 tablespoon	cumin, ground	2 tablespoons	oregano, dried
½ pound	roma tomatoes, whole	1½	bay leaves
3	banana leaves	1	habañero, sliced
¼ cup	garlic cloves, toasted	½ pound	roma tomatoes, sliced
½ cup	achiote paste	2 pounds	yellow onions, sliced
1½	grapefruits, juiced		
2	oranges, juiced		
3	limes, juiced		

Slice the pork shoulder into half-pound slices. Season the pork slices with the salt, pepper and cumin.

Grill the whole tomatoes for just a few minutes to start the caramelization process. Grill the pork lightly for 2 minutes or so per side to caramelize the outside. Grill the banana leaves for just a few seconds and place in the bottom of a roasting pan lined with enough foil to later enclose the pork in the banana leaves. Place the meat on top of the banana leaves.

In a small sauté pan, lightly fry the garlic cloves in a small amount of olive oil, just until they start to brown. Remove the garlic cloves from the pan immediately or they will continue to cook.

Preheat the oven to 350°F.

Blend the garlic, achiote paste, citrus juices, vinegar, oregano, bay leaves and habañero. Cover the meat with the blended mixture. Slice the grilled tomatoes. Put the fresh sliced tomatoes, the grilled tomatoes and the onions on top of the pork. Wrap in the banana leaves, then double wrap in foil. Make sure it's airtight. Bake for 3½ hours.

PICKLED ONIONS

2 each	red onions	1 teaspoon	sugar
¼ cup	grapefruit juice	¼ teaspoon	kosher salt
1 tablespoon	orange juice	pinch	black pepper
½ teaspoon	lemon juice	½	habañero, sliced
¼ teaspoon	lime juice	2 tablespoons	olive oil
2 tablespoons	red wine vinegar		

Thinly slice the onions and set aside. Bring the citrus juices, vinegar, sugar, salt, pepper and habañero slices to a boil. Remove from heat, allow to cool. Toss the onions and olive oil together and cover with the pickling liquid. Cover and refrigerate overnight.

GRAPEFRUIT MARGARITA

YIELD: 1 SERVING

½	grapefruit, juiced
1½ ounces	tequila
1 ounce	sweet & sour, fresh*
1 tablespoon	simple syrup
1 tablespoon	agave nectar

Combine all the ingredients into a shaker with ice. Shake vigorously for 10 seconds.

FRESH SWEET & SOUR

1 ounce	lime, juiced
1 ounce	lemon, juiced
1 ounce	simple syrup

Combine all ingredients.

El Hidalguense began as a typical Mexican restaurant where fajitas and chicken were the focus. On occasion, the owners would cook a dish originating from the Huasteca region of Mexico for themselves and curious customers would request a taste. When those customers returned, they would frequently request these off-the-menu items. Before long, the demand was higher for more of these recipes than Tex-Mex food, making El Hidalguense a legendary source for truly authentic regional Mexican cuisine.

EL HIDALGUENSE
CABRITO ENCHILADO

For fans of cabrito, the preparation at El Hidalguense is considered the benchmark for goat cooking. The skin on their cabrito asado is crisp and the meat is so tender and juicy it slides effortlessly off the bone. Their cabrito enchilado, featured here, is spicier, equally delicious and easily cooked in the oven.

YIELD: 10 SERVINGS

5 pounds	cabrito	2 tablespoons	black pepper
¾ pound	guajillo chiles	2	bay leaves
1	onion, medium	2 tablespoons	thyme
3	garlic cloves	½ tablespoon	salt (more to taste)
2 tablespoons	cumin	¼ to ½ cup	water

Preheat your oven to 300˚F.

Rinse off the cabrito and place it into a roasting pan.

Wash and dry the chiles, making sure to remove the seeds and membranes.

Soak the chiles in hot water for at least 1 hour. Place the chiles in a blender and puree.

Next, mince the onion and garlic and add to the blender. Then, add the cumin, pepper, bay leaves, thyme, salt and water. Blend until liquefied.

Pour the mixture over the cabrito. Cover the roasting pan with aluminum foil.

Place in the oven and bake for 2 to 3 hours.

Garnish with lime wedges, chopped cilantro and onions.

ALICIA'S MEXICAN GRILLE
ALAMBRES

Alambres are, simply put, Mexican shish-kabobs. But, with the addition of shrimp, peppers and bacon, this version really sends a traditional dish over the moon. For a little extra 'kick', thread some whole jalapeños randomly onto the skewers as well. Be sure to marinate the beef for a minimum of 15 minutes but no more than an hour. The soy sauce will break down the meat very quickly and longer marinating will produce a mushy texture.

YIELD: 8 SERVINGS

3 pounds	beef tenderloin		1	white onion, large
1 pound	bacon, sliced		8	mushrooms
3	green bell peppers		16	shrimp, large, peeled
2	red bell peppers			& deveined

MARINADE

1 cup	soy sauce		½ cup	water
1 cup	worcestershire sauce			

Combine all the marinade ingredients. Submerge the tenderloin cubes in the marinade for a minimum of 15 minutes.

Pre-cook the bacon to medium before cutting into 2-inch pieces.

Slice the green and red bell pepper into 1½-inch pieces. Cut the onions into 2-inch pieces. Slice the mushrooms in half.

The perfect alambre is threaded like this:

> green pepper, meat, onion, bacon, mushroom, shrimp, red pepper, meat, onion, bacon, mushroom, shrimp, green pepper, meat and finish with the onion.

Brush a small amount of vegetable oil on the alambres. Sear the alambres on a plancha or on a grill. Be sure to rotate to sear evenly.

Remove the alambres and place them in a shallow roasting pan. Cover with foil and bake for about 5 to 10 minutes or when an internal temperature of 145˚F is reached.

Reserve the juices from the roasting pan and pour over the alambres before serving.

Raised on his grandfather's farm in El Salvador, David Herrera came to the U.S. with a prodigal knowledge of fresh meats, vegetables and herbs. Speaking not a single word of English, he migrated here at the age of eighteen and was immediately drawn to the restaurant business. Seven years later he became front waiter at Tony Vallone's upscale restaurant, Anthony's. Determined to excel, he knew he needed spot-on descriptive skills to entice the diners so he spent hours with the chefs learning the techniques, tastes and the art of plate presentation. Today, he uses those same skills to 'wow' folks in his own establishments.

Herrera's upscale American Bistro and Steakhouse, Dario's, is right next door to one of Alicia's two locations and reaps the benefits of its close proximity. The end cuts of the house-butchered meats are the source for the fork-tender beef that is featured in this alambres dish and their fajitas as well.

CIELO MEXICAN BISTRO
JALAPEÑO GLAZED SNAPPER

This beautifully presented dish is a favorite at lovely Cielo in the heart of downtown Houston. Served whole, this impressive fish is glazed in a sweet, jalapeño balsamic reduction, topped with chopped pistachios and tastes as incredible as it looks. Use the best quality, aged balsamic vinegar you can afford for the best results and make sure your skillet is really hot to sear in the amazing flavors and to properly cook through.

Owner and Chef Hicham Nafaa is masterful with fish due in large part to his years spent in Hawaii. He returned to Houston to create a concept restaurant that felt like a vacation spot, to spectacular effect. The restaurant interiors are cavernous but warm and well-appointed and diners can easily forget about the bustling metropolis whizzing by outside while salivating over entrees like poblano-glazed sea scallops, open-faced tamales and chile-glazed pork ribs.

WHITE SANGRIA

½	orange, juiced
1 bottle	white wine, dry
2 tablespoons	sugar
1 ounce	brandy
1 ounce	Cointreau
½	orange, thinly sliced
1	lemon, thinly sliced
1	peach, thinly sliced
2 cups	ice cubes
1 cup	club soda

Combine the orange juice, wine, sugar, brandy and Cointreau. Add the lemon and orange slices. Chill. To serve, add ice and club soda and stir gently.

YIELD: 2 TO 4 SERVINGS

JALAPEÑO GLAZE

1 cup	balsamic vinegar	½ cup	chipotles (canned), blended
1 cup	sugar	½ cup	cilantro, chopped
¼ cup	soy sauce	½ cup	maple syrup

Combine all the ingredients in a small saucepan and bring to a boil. Reduce the temperature and simmer for 1 to 2 hours, until very thick.

SNAPPER

1½ to 2 pounds	snapper, whole	⅛ cup	pistachios, peeled and roasted
¼ cup	olive oil		

Preheat the oven to 350°F.

Make sure the fish is cleaned, scaled and the fins are removed.

Add the olive oil to a sauté pan over medium-high heat. Add the fish and cook for about 5 minutes per side. Next, generously brush the glaze onto the fish and top with the pistachios after roughly chopping them.

Place in the oven for about 5 minutes or until cooked through. Serve with the remaining glaze on the side.

TILA'S
CHILE EN NOGADA

This is a celebratory dish from the state of Puebla, the colors of which represent the Mexican Flag. It is said to have been first served on August 21, 1821, when Mexico defeated the French. It can be served hot or cold and can even be battered and fried, if you like. There are a lot of ingredients here, but the outcome will be well worth your efforts.

YIELD: 8 SERVINGS

8	poblano peppers, roasted, seeded, & deveined
1 tablespoon	butter, unsalted
4 tablespoons	olive oil
½	onion, finely chopped
2 tablespoons	garlic, minced
1 pound	chicken, turkey, beef, pork or ham, ground
¾ cup	raisins
¼ cup	apricots, dried
⅓ cup	candied citron
1	pear, large
1	peach, large
1	apple
½ cup	pineapple
1	mango

¾ pound	tomatoes
¼ tablespoon	cinnamon, ground
1 pinch	cloves, ground
1 pinch	nutmeg, ground
2	bay leaves
1	thyme sprig
1 teaspoon	black pepper, ground
1 tablespoon	chile pesto*
¼ cup	sherry, dry
¼ cup	white wine, dry
½ cup	chicken bouillon
to taste	salt
2	pomegranates, seeds from
1 bunch	cilantro or parsley, chopped

In a saucepan, heat the butter and the olive oil over medium-high heat. Add the onion and garlic and cook until lightly browned. Add the ground meat and cook until all of the redness disappears.

Finely chop the raisins, apricots, citron, pear, peach, apple, pineapple, mango and tomatoes, then add to the meat mixture and stir to combine. Next, add the cinnamon, cloves, nutmeg, bay leaves, thyme, pepper, chile pesto, sherry, wine, chicken bouillon and salt to taste.

Reduce the heat and simmer, constantly stirring until thick and the flavors are well blended. Set aside to cool. Next, fill the chiles with the cooled stuffing. Put the chiles on a sheet pan, cover with foil and refrigerate until ready to cook.

Preheat the oven to 350˚F. Remove the sheet pan of chiles from the refrigerator and cover with aluminum foil.

Place the sheet pan in the oven and cook until hot, about 30 to 45 minutes.

Place the peppers on plates or a platter. Ladle the nut sauce on top. Sprinkle with the pomegranate seeds and garnish with parsley or cilantro.

The leftover stuffing and sauce can be used for empanadas, quesadillas, tacos, etc.

NUT SAUCE

¼ cup	goat cheese
1 teaspoon	tarragon
1 teaspoon	parsley
1 teaspoon	garlic, roasted & chopped
to taste	salt & pepper
1 cup	walnuts, roasted, ground
1 cup	almonds, roasted, ground
½ cup	cashews, roasted, ground
7 tablespoons	cream cheese
¼ cup	queso fresco
¼ slice	wheat bread, soaked in milk, no crust
½ cup	heavy cream
¾ cup	milk (if too thick add more)
1 teaspoon	white onions, grated
¼ teaspoon	cinnamon, ground
2 tablespoons	sherry, dry
to taste	salt

Season the goat cheese with the tarragon, parsley and garlic. Add salt and pepper to taste. Add the goat cheese and remaining ingredients in a saucepan over medium heat. Let simmer until flavors are well combined.

CHILE PESTO

2 cups	serranos, roasted
1 tablespoon	garlic, roasted, chopped
2 tablespoons	white onion, chopped
⅓ pound	roma tomatoes, roasted
¾ teaspoon	chicken bouillon powder
1 teaspoon	salt
¾ teaspoon	cilantro, chopped
1 tablespoon	olive oil

Remove the serrano stems and process all the ingredients (except the oil) in a food processor. Sauté the mixture in olive oil for about 15 minutes until the extra liquid is reduced.

TAMARINDO AGUA FRESCA

20	tamarind pods
2 quarts	water
1½ cups	sugar

Peel the tamarind pods, removing the veins that run along the sides. Leave the seeds.

In a saucepan, bring the water to a boil and add peeled tamarind pods. Boil over high heat until the pods are soft, about 20 minutes.

Remove from the heat and with the back of a spoon, mash the softened pods against the side of the pan.

When cool, strain mixture thoroughly, add the sugar, ice and enjoy.

EL BOLILLO BAKERY
OJARASCAS

The Wedding Cookie is a special occasion cookie that is also served at holidays. It became popular as a wedding treat because at such an auspicious occasion, hosts wanted to serve something extra special. Traditionally, they were made of the finest and most expensive ingredients they could budget. I have always wanted a good recipe for these little gems and this one is amazing.

When I was testing this recipe, Kirk Michaels reminded me to add some Beback Powder to the dough before baking. A look of confusion crossed my face and he began to laugh. He gave no explanation. It wasn't until I tasted his amazing baked samples when I got home... I realized that one taste of his yummy little cookies and he can be fairly certain you'll 'be back' to his marvelous bakery.

YIELD: 2 TO 3 DOZEN COOKIES

2	eggs	1 tablespoon	baking powder
1 cup	sugar	1 tablespoon	cinnamon (coarse ground)
½ pound	shortening		
1 teaspoon	vanilla extract	for kneading	flour
¼ teaspoon	almond extract	for dusting	cinnamon & sugar
3 cups	flour		

Preheat the oven to 350˚F.

In a large bowl, blend the eggs, sugar and shortening until well combined. Next, add the vanilla and almond extracts and mix well.

In a separate bowl, combine the flour, baking powder and cinnamon and mix together.

Add the flour mixture, about 1 cup at a time, blending well.

Turn the mixture out onto a floured cutting board or counter. Knead a few times with generously floured hands until manageable.

Roll the dough into quarter-sized balls and place them on a baking pan.

Put in the oven and bake for about 18 minutes.

While the cookies are still warm, place them into a bowl or bag of a cinnamon and sugar mixture. Toss until completely covered.

REBECCA MASSON
DOS LECHES Y CANELA FLAN

Pastry Chef Rebecca Masson enjoys near cult status in Houston. Her inventive creations grace the menus of such notable eateries as Ibiza, Stella Sola and *17 at the Alden. The Le Cordon Bleu trained master was voted Pastry Chef of the year by My Table Magazine in 2007. More recently, she outshined all the savory-focused chefs at the Houston Chowhounds 'Shroom Throwdown with her Candy Cap Ice Box Pie. Once again, she surpasses any expectations you might have about a dessert. This flan is phenomenal.

YIELD: 8 SERVINGS

CARAMEL

1 cup	sugar	1 tablespoon	corn syrup, light
½ cup	water		

Combine all the ingredients in a saucepan and cook until golden amber. Pour into the bottom of each of the ramekins and give them a good swirl to coat.

CUSTARD

14 ounces	sweetened condensed milk	8	egg yolks
24 ounces	evaporated milk	½ teaspoon	vanilla extract

Preheat oven to 325°F.

Combine all the ingredients in a large bowl. Use a hand blender to mix. Set aside.

Pour the milk mixture over the caramelized sugar in ramekins.

Place the ramekins in a roasting pan and place the pan on the center oven rack. Add hot water halfway up the sides of the roasting pan, being careful not to spill into the ramekins. Cover the roasting pan with foil and gently slide into the oven.

Bake for 1 hour or until the edges are set. When you slightly jiggle the roasting pan, the custard will shake like jello. Remove from the oven and let the ramekins sit in the water until slightly cool. Next, remove the ramekins from the water and place on a wire rack to cool completely. Cover and chill at least 8 hours.

COFFEE WHIPPED CREAM

2 cups	heavy whipping cream	1 tablespoon	coffee extract
2 tablespoons	powdered sugar		

Whip everything together in a stand mixer with whisk attachment. Whip until stiff peaks form and chill.

To plate, run a knife around the edge of the ramekins and invert onto a plate. Set a katafi disk on top of the flan and then place a quenelle of the coffee-whipped cream on top. Serve immediately.

CINNAMON KATAFI

¼ package	katafi (shredded phyllo)
4 tablespoons	butter, unsalted, melted
¼ cup	powdered sugar
1 tablespoon	ground cinnamon

Carefully separate the katafi. You don't have to separate it completely, just enough to look like jumbled up spaghetti. Toss the butter, sugar and cinnamon with the katafi. Pull out a small handful and arrange in a circle (should be ¼-inch thick,) on a sheet pan lined with parchment paper. Continue until you have used all the katafi. You will want to make extras, they break easily. Top with another sheet of parchment and another sheet pan. Bake at 350°F for about 10 minutes. Remove the top sheet pan and parchment paper and continue baking until golden brown, about 6 to 8 minutes more.

Teotihuacán
Mexican Café

This is also a 'two-for-one' recipe, as you'll begin by making flour tortillas from scratch. But don't let that discourage you, because you're in good hands. Silvia Galvan, the owner and Chef at Teotihuacan, is known as the Tortilla Queen of Houston and her foolproof recipe will amaze you. Your homemade tortillas will be as good as the best you've ever eaten.

Texas Monthly's 2004 issue of the "Insiders Guide to Mexican Food" named Zagat-rated Teotihuacan's fajitas the best in town. And, I can tell you that everything I have ever eaten there has been phenomenal. The parillada (a mixed platter of grilled meats) is a favorite of diners as are the shrimp and scallop enchiladas which are served in a velvety cream sauce. Spicy food lovers can't get enough of the bacon-wrapped caliente camarones. And, the chicken and cheese flautas are...to-die-for! I'm especially in love with an off-the-menu special of carne asada topped with mushrooms, spinach, white cheese and onions.

This restaurant cranks out unbelievable food and won't break the (your) bank!

TEOTIHUACAN
Sopapillas

Sopapillas are another dish that many regions lay claim to. Although they are thought to have originated in New Mexico over 200 years ago, they are derived from old Spanish cuisine.

This puffy, fried pastry is both crispy and a little chewy and gets its sweet finish from a 'roll' in a cinnamon and sugar mixture.

YIELD: 12 SOPAPILLAS OR TORTILLAS

TORTILLAS

2½ cups	flour	⅔ cup	water, hot
½ cup	shortening	for frying	vegetable oil
2¼ teaspoons	baking powder	for dusting	cinnamon & sugar
1½ teaspoons	salt		

Combine the flour, baking powder and salt in a medium bowl. Be sure to mix well.

Cut the shortening into large cubes and add to the bowl. Mix the shortening into the flour mixture with your hands. Pea-sized bits of shortening that remain are ideal.

Heat the water in a small saucepan to 160˚F. (This is a very important detail.)

Add the water, in small increments, mixing well, to form a dough ball. Be sure not to over-mix.

Divide the dough into 12 equal-sized balls. Sprinkle a little flour onto the counter or a large cutting or pastry board. Using a floured rolling pin, roll the balls into thin, round tortillas.

Fold the tortillas in half, then roll out again. Slice or cut into whatever shape or size you like and trim off any rough ends (a pizza cutter works nicely.)

Heat the oil to 375˚F in a deep skillet or stockpot. Add the folded, rolled tortilla and fry for 1 to 2 minutes per side.

Dust each sopapilla with cinnamon and sugar. Serve with honey.

Recipe Note: If you only want to make flour tortillas, simply cook the tortillas in a dry skillet over medium-high heat for about 45 seconds, or until the top starts to bubble. Then flip the tortilla and cook for an additional 45 seconds.

TEOTIHUACAN MEXICAN RICE

4 cups	chicken broth
1 tablespoon	garlic
¼ cup	onions
1½	tomatoes, medium
1½ tablespoons	corn oil
2 cups	long grain rice
½ tablespoon	salt
½ tablespoon	chicken bouillon
½ cup	bell pepper, chopped
½ cup	carrots, grated
½ can	sweet corn mix (not creamed)

Bring the chicken broth to a boil in a stockpot. Remove 1 cup of the broth and blend with the garlic, onions and tomatoes.

In a saucepan, heat the corn oil over medium heat. When hot, add the rice, and stir until light brown.

Next, add the salt, chicken bouillon, bell pepper, carrots, corn and blended chicken broth. Add the remaining chicken both and bring to a boil.

Cover with a lid and lower the heat. Simmer for 10 minutes. Remove the lid and let cook for 3 more minutes to allow the remaining liquid to evaporate. Fluff with a fork. Makes 4 cups of rice.

SOLERO'S NOPALITOS SALAD

1 (30 oz.) jar	nopalitos
1 tablespoon	red onion
1 tablespoon	garlic, minced
2 tablespoons	goat cheese
	cilantro dressing*

Drain the nopalitos and rinse well. Julienne the red onion and finely chop the garlic. In a large bowl, combine the nopalitos, red onion and garlic and stir well. Next, crumble the goat cheese and add to the salad. Add the cilantro dressing, toss and garnish with yellow and red tomato and a cilantro sprig. Serves 4.

CILANTRO DRESSING

1 tablespoon	mustard
1 tablespoon	cilantro
1 tablespoon	lemon juice
pinch	cumin
2 tablespoons	orange juice
1 tablespoon	cilantro leaves
½ cup	olive oil

Put all ingredients in a blender, except the oil. Blend, then add the oil in a stream to emulsify.

BESO'S CALABACITAS

1 tablespoon	extra virgin olive oil
1	onion, medium, chopped
1	poblano or serrano, seeded & diced
2 cups	zucchini, diced
2 cups	summer squash, diced
1/2 cup	corn, fresh off the cob
1 tablespoon	garlic, minced
1/2 teaspoon	salt
2 tablespoons	cilantro, chopped

Heat the oil in a large, nonstick skillet over medium heat. Add the onion and chile and cook, stirring until soft, about 6 minutes. Add the zucchini, summer squash, corn and salt. Cover and cook for about 10 to 15 minutes or until tender, stirring a few times. Remove from the heat and stir in cilantro. Serves 4 to 6.

TILA'S SALSA ROJA

1¼ pounds	tomatoes, roasted
2¼ tablespoons	serranos, roasted
⅛ pound	white onion
⅜ teaspoon	garlic, crushed
2¼ tablespoons	cilantro
1⅛ teaspoons	lime juice
⅝ teaspoon	salt
⅝ teaspoon	chicken base paste
⅓ teaspoon	olive oil

Combine all the ingredients (except the oil) in a food processor and chop. Put in a pan with olive oil and simmer for about 30 minutes. Adjust salt to taste. Makes 4 cups.

NINFA'S FAMOUS GREEN SALSA

2 pounds	green tomatoes
¼ pound	tomatillos
½ cup	guacamole
½ teaspoon	garlic powder
1 each	jalapeños, fresh, fried
½ tablespoons	cilantro
6 tablespoons	sour cream
6 tablespoons	water
to taste	kosher salt

Roast the tomatillos and tomatoes until lightly charred on top. Cool.

Then blend with all the remaining ingredients, except the water. With the blender running, add the water to reach the desired consistency. Season to taste with salt. Makes 4 cups.

Index

100% TAQUITO	43	EL TIEMPO	63	OLIVETTE	19
1308 CANTINA	23	ENCHILADA SPICING SAUCE	54	ORIGINAL NINFA'S, THE	79
AGUA DE MELÓN	51	ESCALANTE'S	35	ORTEGA, HUGO	39
ALAMBRES	83	EVERTS, JEFF	19	PALOMA COCKTAIL	47
ALDIS, ERIC	15	FARB, CAROLYN	15	PAPPASITO'S	20
ALICIA'S MEXICAN GRILLE	83	FISH TACOS	28	PICA RITA	27
ANAYA, CAROLYN	57	FLAUTAS DE LEAH	36	PICO DE GALLO	39
ANAYA, CYCLONE & CAROLINA	57	FRESH SWEET & SOUR	12, 20	PORK BELLY AL PASTOR TORTA	64
ANOMAIPRASERT, TEAL & SURIN	64	GALVAN, IRMA	60	QUESO FLAMEADO	44
APRICOT SUNRISE	39	GARCIA FAMILY	44	RDG + BAR ANNIE	47
AVOCADO MARGARITA	28	GRAPEFRUIT MARGARITA	79	RED CABBAGE SLAW	28
BECERRA, POLO	27	GRINGO'S MEXICAN KITCHEN	71	REFRIED BLACK BEANS	39
BERRYHILL BAJA GRILL	58	GUACAMOLE	11, 15	RODRIGUEZ, CESAR	68
BESO	16	GUACAMOLE SALSA	36	ROMERO'S LAS BRAZAS	36
BLACK OLIVE PURÉE	11	GUACAMOLE RELISH	15	SABORES	51
BLACK SAUCE	63	HABAÑEROS MEX GRILL	27	SADLER, BILL	16
BOADA, ARTURO	16	HATCH GREEN CHILE SAUCE	40	SALSA RANCHERA	60
BORRACHO BEANS	63	HAVEN	64	SALSA ROJA	94
CABRITO ENCHILADO	80	HOLT, JUDSON	75	SALSA VERDE	43
CAMARONES DIABLOS	32	HOLT, PETER	75	SANGRIA DEL MESON	44
CAMPECHANA	27	HOLT, STAN & AUDREY	75	SANGRITA	48
CARNE ASADA	63	HORCHATA	68	SANTOS	67
CARNE GUISADA	71	HUACHINANGO VERACRUZANA	72	SHRIMP & MUSHROOM QUESADILLA	35
CARNITAS	67	HUGO'S	39	SHRIMP TAMALES	48
CAROLYN FARB GUACAMOLE	15	IRMA'S	60	SKINNY MARGARITA	57
CASARES, SYLVIA	54	IRMA'S FAMOUS LEMONADE	60	SOPA DE POBLANO	12
CEVICHE	16	JALAPEÑO GLAZE	84	SOPAPILLAS	92
CHARDONNAY SAUCE	57	JALAPEÑO GLAZED SNAPPER	84	SOPESITOS ESPECIALES	51
CHICKEN TORTILLA SOUP	20	JULIA'S BISTRO	31	SOUTHWEST CAESAR SALAD	19
CHILE PESTO	87	LA GUADALUPANA	53	SPANISH FLOWERS	24
CHILE RELLENO	60	LAMB BARBACOA	40	SPICE MIX	15, 63
CHILES EN NOGADA	87	LA PARRANDA	28	STEAK BURRITO	40
CHIPOTLE CHICKEN	68	LAS VENTANAS	72	SYLVIA'S ENCHILADA KITCHEN	54
CHIPOTLE COSTILLAS	75	LA VIDA LOCAL	64	SYLVIA'S SALSA ROJA	54
CHIVE OIL	11	LOBSTER ENCHILADAS	57	TACO MILAGRO	48
CHUY'S	40	LUPE TORTILLA	75	TACOS A GO-GO	40
CIELO MEXICAN BISTRO	84	MANGO JICAMA SALAD	23	TACOS AL PASTOR	43
COCHINITA PIBIL	79	MANGO MARGARITA	35	TAMARINDO AGUA FRESCA	88
CORN TORTILLAS	43	MASSON, REBECCA	91	TEALA'S	32
CRAB MEAT TOSTADAS	47	MAYO-CHIPOTLE SAUCE	28	TEOTIHUACAN	92
CREAM SAUCE	31	MEXICAN RICE	94	TILA'S	87
CREPAS DE HUITLACOCHE	31	MICHELADA	23	TOMATILLO SAUCE	58
CREPE SHELLS	31	MILLS, JIM	19	TURKEY POZOLE	24
CYCLONE ANAYA'S	57	MOJO DE AJO	39	VERACRUZANA SAUCE	72
DEL GRANDE, ROBERT	48	MOLINA'S	12	VERDE CHICKEN ENCHILADAS	58
DONERAKI	68	MORELIA ENCHILADAS	54	WATERMELON MARGARITA	20
DON RAUL MARGARITA	12	MO'S - A PLACE FOR STEAKS	15	WHITE SANGRIA	84
DOS LECHES Y CANELA FLAN	91	NINFA'S FAMOUS GREEN SALSA	94	WILEY, L.J.	11
EL BOLILLO BAKERY	88	NOPALITOS SALAD	94	YELAPA	11
EL HIDALGUENSE	80	NUT SAUCE	87		
EL MESON	44	OJARASCAS	88		

ACKNOWLEDGEMENTS

Are you familiar with the saying, "It takes a village?" Well, it definitely took a village of incredibly talented, hungry folks to put this book together.

How fortunate am I that Houston is such a culinary mecca? The opportunity to work with so many immensely talented people is a joy. The fiercely creative and patient chefs and restaurateurs are my personal blessing. Chef Hugo Ortega and Tracy Vaught were more than accomodating, on many occasions. Chef Arturo Boada, once again, went out of his way to help me and his guidance led me to some of the small, very special restaurants featured here. Pay these restaurants a visit. You'll be delighted and your taste buds will appreciate it.

As wonderful as all of the recipes are, without the remarkable photography skills of Billy, my loving and uber-talented husband, this would be just another cookbook. If we can just figure out a way to do a 'scratch and sniff' book that's not cost prohibitive, we'd be rich for certain.

Without the vision of my good friend, Kit Wohl, designer of the *Classic Recipes Series*, *Houston Classic Mexican Recipes* would not have been possible. She's a great advisor and sounding board and I will never be able to thank her enough.

Next to thank is my talented editor, Jeffrey Linthicum. Once again, he knew what I was thinking even when I did not. An awesome writer, artist, food stylist, cook, designer and tailor. Honestly, I'm not sure what he can't do.

There were a few other eyes that helped with the proofreading - special thanks to Diane Hause and Ronna Braselton for their help. Paula Murphy and Carlos Martinez offered invaluable advice and guidance, for which I am very grateful. Yoli Kalkofen of ApronSenorita.com was gracious enough to send me colorful Mexican aprons and dish towels - which definitely helped keep me in a festive recipe testing mode. All of the recipes were tested in home kitchens in Houston, Corpus Christi, and Encino, Texas. Once again, I was blessed with wonderful friends who were willing and even anxious to help translate and test recipes. Thanks to Denise Hyden, Alana Seal, Lori Dixon-Holland, Cayce Ranton, Lynn Allison, Shannon Bush, Ronna Braselton, Meredith Watten-Jaramillo and Molly Merkle. Thanks to Grandma Patsy, whose generousity has helped to make all this possible. Our favorite neighbors, Jay and Barbara Tomek, opened their kitchen to us for multiple photo shoots and they are much appreciated. And then there's that mother-in-law of mine…Mother Miller. She is truly an inspiration and always keeps me stocked with the best kitchen gadgetry, cookbooks and cast iron skillets. Thank you, thank you, thank you.

I own up to any errors and encourage you to contact me via Pelican Publishing with any comments or questions, or visit me on Facebook.

And finally, thanks to the great team at Pelican Publishing: Dr. Milburn Calhoun, Nina Kooij, Terry Callaway, Katie Szadziewicz, and John Scheyd. Here's to selling a million copies.

Most of all, thanks to the booksellers, whose hard work brings kitchen goodness.

Eat like no one is watching.